# Praise f

*Spiritual Problems of Co*

Steve Wilkes has brought to light a dilemma that is all too common and seldom discussed. In SPIRITUAL PROBLEMS OF COMMITTED CHRISTIANS Wilkes discusses with candor the issues of discouragement, doubt, lust, fear and others that badger the most dedicated follower of Christ. Saturated with Scripture and filled with candid personal illustrations with which the reader will readily identify, the book goes on to offer solutions to overcoming these problems and claiming the victory we have been given in Christ.

—JERRY RANKIN
President Emeritus
International Mission Board, SBC

No matter how spiritual you become, you will be attacked by temptation. And remember, Satan knows your weaknesses and will try to get to you anyway he can. Steve Wilkes has written a book on the temptations that beset the committed Christian; but he does not to stop there, he shows how to overcome temptations, to keep ones commitment strong, and to be victorious over sin. May you become more committed to Jesus Christ as a result of reading this book, and may you accomplish more in servicing Christ.

—ELMER L. TOWNS
Co-Founder and Vice President
Liberty University
Lynchburg, Virginia

# Praise for

## *Spiritual Problems of Committed Christians*

More pastors would be in the ministry today if they were required to read Steve Wilkes' timely book! Wilkes tackles the temptations that most church leaders will encounter, giving honest and helpful advice on each. This may the one book next to the Bible that every church leader should be required to read!

—BOB WHITSEL, D.MIN., PH.D.
*author of nine books on leadership*
Professor of Missional Leadership
Wesley Seminary
Indiana Wesleyan University

Have you ever struggled with doubt, or discouragement, or maybe even bitterness? All Christians, even the most committed ones it seems, face challenges in living a vibrant Christian life. Now, Steve Wilkes, in his new book Spiritual Problems of Committed Christians unwraps the mystery of following Christ with passion and vitality. He defines what a committed Christian really is, and offers insights on how to live daily for and with Christ. It's a book every Christian needs to read and put into practice. I know I'm going to, and you should too.

—GARY L. MCINTOSH, PH.D.
Professor of Christian Ministry & Leadership
Talbot School of Theology
Biola University

# Praise for

## *Spiritual Problems of Committed Christians*

I've had the joy of serving with Dr. Steve Wilkes in the same department for 15 years; he's writing about his passion and his life. The truths this book presents flow from his life experience both as a pastor and a professor who loves, influences, and helps novice (and some not so new) pastors and missionaries. You'll read his work with pleasure and profit.

—STAN MAY, PH.D.
Chairman and Professor
Missions Department
Mid-America Baptist Theological Seminary

The words "informative, concise, practical, and redemptive" all come to mind as I read the pages of this book. The issues presented in these pages face every believer in some way every day. Dr. Wilkes has captured the pulse of practical Christian living as he presents the problems, addresses the devastation caused by the problem, and then brings a Biblical solution to the problem. As a pastor I intend to recommend this work to every believer as both a handbook and a counseling tool in ministerial life. I sense the value of this work will last far beyond all of our expectations. Thank you Bro. Steve for your sensitivity and concern for the battles faced daily in the spiritual realm.

—WAYNE MARSHALL
Senior Pastor
Longview Heights Baptist Church
Olive Branch, MS

# *Spiritual* PROBLEMS *of Committed Christians*

# Spiritual *of Committed Christians* Problems

Steve Wilkes

BorderStone Press, LLC

2011

First American Edition

*Spiritual Problems of Committed Christians*

Author: Steve Wilkes

Edited by Roger D. Duke
Cover design by Tim Spencer

Published by BorderStone Press, LLC, PO Box 1383, Mountain Home, AR 72654
Dallas, TX / Memphis, TN

www.borderstonepress.com



Supervising editor: Brian Mooney
Consulting editor: Bradley Mooney



ISBN: 978-1-936670-04-8

Library of Congress Control Number: 2010943476

# Contents

# Acknowledgements

I would like to thank several key people who helped me make this book a reality.

Meredith Tipton, my wonderful daughter, who is also my official editorial assistant, sentence re-writer, and helper. You are the best and your writing skills are almost unsurpassed.

Cathy Rech, my secretary at the Seminary, for your constant help in typing, and your encouragement.

Dr. Stan May for reading and making great suggestions on the entire manuscript. Your skill with words and proper form is great, but your servant heart is even greater.

To my lovely and wonderful wife Carol for all of your encouragement to write and publish. There is none like you!

To Mid-America Baptist Theological Seminary for allowing me to take and a Sabbatical to write and for maintaining an atmosphere that encourages me to write and stretch myself for Jesus.

To our wonderful Lord Jesus for His love, acceptance, and power as we serve Him. May He be praised here and for all eternity!

# What is a Committed Christian?

I HAVE A DREAM! It is that Christians will be sold out to Jesus and live like it. I am weary of people saying they are committed Christians but nobody would know it.

Some people assume that because people are born again that they are actually committed Christians; however, that is not true. Some Christians are committed, and some Christians are not committed to Jesus. In fact, perhaps more than half of those who are saved are not committed to the lordship of Jesus Christ in their daily lives.

By reading this book, I assume that you want what I want—you want to be a truly committed Christian. Honestly, it is the only way you can be used by God and enjoy the Christian life.

I became a Christian when I was in high school, and for most of my high school years I tried to live for Jesus. I began to learn a little about sharing my faith, and I had the joy of winning 2 or 3 people to Jesus before I was out of high school. Then at the end of my senior year, Carol came into my life and I fell in love. At that time when I was 18 and on top of the world, I fell head over heels in love. Something began to happen very subtly in my spiritual life. I didn't perceive it or plan it.

Slowly but surely, Jesus was no longer my passion or my Lord. Somehow I, and my relationship with Carol, took that position.

At the beginning of my second semester in college, I had a strange experience that troubled me. I was sitting on my bunk one day, and I decided to open my Bible and read it. I had not been reading my Bible regularly. I began to read and something stopped me; I just could not read it. I'm not saying this was the work of the devil, rather it seemed to be the work of the flesh, my flesh and my old nature. Jesus was no longer in charge of my life spiritually, and it was showing in a dramatic way.

I stayed away from the Lord most of my first two years of college. I transferred to the University of Alabama for my second year of college (where Carol was attending). I took a history course that spring with a student named Randy. Randy had been the Christian leader at my high school. By our sophomore year, he may have been the top Christian leader at Alabama. He and I studied together once or twice, and he invited me to a Bible study on Tuesday nights at 9:00. It was held in a girl's dormitory on the campus at Alabama. Soon, Carol and I went to this Bible study together. This was in the early spring of our sophomore year, and I was still away from God.

The first week we went to the Bible study there were about 30 college kids attending. The study was led by Howard Borland, a Presbyterian elder from Briarwood Presbyterian Church in Birmingham. Mr. Borland was an accountant in his fifties. He taught the Word of God with power. He talked about how he and his wife, Dixie, had recently won people to Jesus. All of this came crashing down on my heart, and I gave my life fully and completely back to Jesus to be my Lord that night. Two years was more than long enough to be away from Him. It was almost like I had been saved once again. I had a hunger for the Bible, I wanted to be around Christians, I wanted to share my faith, and I wanted to live a holy life. The difference was who was the boss in my heart. When I was living like a normal college student, I was the boss of my heart. When I surrendered to Jesus afresh, He became Lord of my heart again, and things changed.

Perhaps I have been talking about your life, and you are now living with Jesus as the boss, ruler, master, or Lord of your life. If you are congratulations! You are a rare breed. You're part of that born-again army which can help win our world to Jesus Christ. You really are special.

Early in my journey with Jesus, I discovered the verse in Romans 12:1 that states, "Therefore, I urge you, brothers, in view of God's mercy, to offer your bodies as living sacrifices, holy and pleasing to God—this is your spiritual act of worship." I'm sure I did not understand everything about this verse and all its implications, but I did understand as a young Christian that God wanted me to give my body to Him as a living sacrifice and to regularly surrender all that I am to Jesus Christ. Scripture says that this is pleasing to God, and it is my spiritual act of worship. That's what I want to do in the Christian life—to please God and worship Him in a spiritual way.

Committed Christians still have spiritual problems. Many think that once we have surrendered our lives to Jesus as Lord, our spiritual problems would all be solved. However, such is not the case. We have to learn to deal with bitterness, discouragement, and with relationship problems. These problems don't go away when we surrender to Jesus Christ as Lord. This volume will discuss the company of the committed and how to handle our spiritual problems.

Keep reading. The following chapters discuss the problems of committed Christians, now that we have defined what a committed Christian really is. If you are not a committed Christian, this is the best time possible to change. I am not suggesting it can happen instantly. I'm suggesting that if you will get your heart clean before God and confess all known sin, then you're in a position to surrender everything to Jesus afresh. Do that and you will be ready to grow as you learn about other common spiritual problems of committed Christians.

1

# DISCOURAGEMENT

## *Satan's Master Weapon*

ONE BEAUTIFUL SPRING DAY, I was having my personal devotional time outside on our patio. Things were going well in my own spiritual life and in my ministry, but the year before, I had spent about eight months in extreme frustration and discouragement. Some things had happened the spring before which had dealt me a temporary defeat, and that defeat had led to long term discouragement. For about eight months I had lived under a cloud, and in my heart, I secretly had given up.

This particular day, I was reading Romans 12 in the New International Version. I came across verse 11 (and Paul's list of brief commands) which says, "Never be lacking in zeal, but keep your spiritual fervor, serving the Lord." Suddenly it gripped my heart. At that particular moment I was not lacking in zeal, my spiritual fervor was fine, but I remembered the year before; and it occurred to me for the first time in my life that what had happened the year before, perhaps, was not just a time of weakness or disappointment. Perhaps there was something I could have done about it.

As I began to search the Bible for other thoughts on this same theme, I ran across several other passages which related to the same problem. Paul's writings especially seemed to be full of advice about discouragement and the strong command for the Christian never to give up. The Bible was clear on how to deal with discouragement.

I am firmly persuaded, after 39 years of ministry and 26 years of teaching ministers, that discouragement is the number-one spiritual obstacle committed Christians face. Committed Christians and full-time Christian workers regularly succumb to discouragement and experience a draining of their spiritual power and zeal. Most devotional literature offers very little help in dealing with discouragement. In fact, not once have I read anything which told me that I might need to deal with discouragement as a sin problem that I could do something about. Yet, it is one of Satan's greatest tools. In fact, if the devil can discourage a Christian leader, he can often discourage many of those under the leader's influence. That spring day, however, I began to discover a biblical solution for discouragement. Although no one told me this truth, in my personal quiet time,

God, through His Word, began to give me some handles about dealing with personal discouragement.

## A Description of Discouragement

EXACTLY WHAT IS DISCOURAGEMENT, and how can we know when we are dominated by it? Since we are talking about a problem related to human emotions, it is very difficult to be specific in this area. Discouragement can be identified in different people in different ways. Certainly, it is not discouragement to have a bad day or even a few bad days. It is not discouragement to be disappointed over the reactions of a friend or the failure of a plan. Clinical depression is much different from discouragement. I am certain there is a major difference between the two. Christians gripped by a sense of defeat, who come to the place where they simply want to give up and don't feel like trying any more, are probably experiencing spiritual discouragement.

In Isaiah 50:10-11, the prophet talks about a strange experience that many committed Christians have lived through—some call it the ministry of darkness. The prophet makes it very plain that the people he is talking about are believers in God, but these believers, nonetheless, do experience a time of darkness. This spiritual darkness may be similar to what many modern writers have called spiritual dryness—a time when the spiritual emotions of thrill and excitement simply are not there. The Bible does not speak to your heart. Prayer feels meaningless. Christian service and witnessing are even empty and feel futile. This is spiritual darkness or dryness, though discouragement is somewhat different than darkness.

Although discouragement may be one of the chief tools of Satan, it is not new in his bag of tricks. A quick survey through the Bible reveals that several of the leaders throughout biblical history faced this problem. God warned Joshua as he was preparing to lead the children of Israel across the Jordan River into the Promised Land that he might face discouragement. In Joshua 1:9, the Lord said, “Have I not commanded you? Be strong and courageous. Do not be terrified; do not be discouraged, for the Lord your God will be with you wherever you go.” Moses had died, and Joshua had just taken over leadership of the nation of Israel. An extremely difficult task lay ahead of Joshua. God knew that there were powerful enemies in the land, but that the greatest enemy which Joshua would face would be within his own heart. In verses 6-9 in this chapter, God says repeatedly to Joshua that he must not be afraid—and he must not be discouraged. Things haven’t changed much. The enemies look different today, and circumstances have certainly changed since Joshua’s day, but our greatest enemies as committed Christians are still within our own hearts.

In my life, I have noticed that discouragement can often follow on the heels of great spiritual victories. In fact, since our spiritual lives are so closely linked to our emotional makeup, there is a definite relationship between spiritual victory and spiritual discouragement. When Christians begin to sense that the presence of God has been withdrawn from them and they feel "dry" in their Christian life, discouragement may be lurking around the corner.

After Jonah had seen awakening or revival break out in Nineveh, he begged God to let him die. Spiritual victory had turned into personal discouragement and defeat. Elijah had a similar experience after his victory on Mt. Carmel. He fled from wicked queen Jezebel, sat under a juniper tree, and asked the Lord to let him die. These two prophets of God were not alone in their feelings. Across the years, men and women of God have suffered from the darkness of defeat and discouragement after spiritual victory. You may be a committed Christian who would even die for Jesus Christ, but you may find yourself giving up in the secret place of your heart. You are living with a sigh—far below the promised victory Paul described in the book of Philippians.

## The Sources of Discouragement

WHAT COULD POSSIBLY lead a genuinely committed Christian to be discouraged? I have known some Christians who were so discouraged that they were actually tired of serving God. In my work I get to know many ministers. It is common to discover that they have given up—they are discouraged. Recently, I was teaching a week-long seminar to ten pastors. During the seminar I often share devotional thoughts to begin the day-long sessions. After I had talked about discouragement, I asked the men to bow their heads. Then I asked those who were discouraged to raise their hands. Six of the ten admitted they were discouraged and wanted to deal with it. Three days later I asked them if the discouragement was gone, and three quickly said, "Yes!" One pastor said he had been discouraged, even though he knew of no reason for it.

Of course there are obvious reasons Christians do get discouraged. Major or minor disappointments sometimes discourage us. Tough relationships and hurt feelings often knock us down spiritually. Committed believers may become discouraged when we have our high hopes and dreams for God dashed. Similarly, we get discouraged when we do not live up to our own expectations.

Jim Elliot's life offers a powerful illustration of what discourages committed Christians. Elliot was an outstanding Christian and a leader at Wheaton College just after World War II. He was full of zeal for missions and never seemed to be daunted by difficult circumstances. After he and Elizabeth were married, Jim and four other missionary friends planned to take the gospel to the violent Auca Indians in Ecuador. Jim's enthusiasm can easily be detected by reading just a little in his autobiography. Just before "Operation Auca" began, Elizabeth, writing about Jim, made the following observation:

> But the Enemy of Souls is not easily persuaded to relinquish his hold in any territory. Seeing that his authority in the Auca region was going to be challenged, he soon launched an attack on the challengers. Jim was beset with temptations such as had never before assailed him, and that master-weapon, discouragement, which to my knowledge had held no power over him since his arrival in Ecuador, met him at every turn. A gloom seemed to settle over his spirit in December, and it seemed that battles were being fought which I could not share (Elliot, *Shadow of the Almighty*, 241).

"That master-weapon, discouragement . . ." is such a powerfully correct observation. When Satan can defeat his foes (us) in no other way, he uses discouragement. If he can get us to bite and succumb to the bait, discouragement will defeat committed Christians every time we give in to it.

## The Impact of Discouragement

DISCOURAGEMENT AFFECTS committed Christians in several areas. Of course we are all different, and we react differently. Physically, many believers are sapped and have less energy when discouraged. Emotionally, discouragement robs us of excitement and motivation. It kills our vision, too! Many of my students leave the seminary full of zeal and vision to do great things for God. Something then knocks them down and their vision is gone. Why? Because discouragement has taken over. Discouragement and vision do not make good bedfellows.

During one of my pastorates, our youth minister and I had a dream to reach un-churched young people through a coffee-house ministry in a storefront we had located. Somehow the word spread in our church that we were planning to target black youth. We were not—we planned to try to reach all types of youth. The deacons had real clout in that church, and they overwhelmingly voted that we could not even try a coffee-house. The impact of the vote was devastating; it discouraged me and stole my zeal. My problem was not the response of the deacons. My problem was that I had not learned how to deal with discouragement in a spiritual manner.

Not only does discouragement affect the committed Christian in his physical, emotional, and spiritual well-being, it can also have a profound effect on his church. That's right, entire churches can actually have a spirit of discouragement. This spirit or attitude can affect a church in dramatic ways, including growth. Some years ago, I visited a church which was pastored by an old friend of mine, where I also had preached previously. Since I had preached there, two small congregations had merged and the merged church was struggling to grow. As I drove to the service, a strange thing happened—God showed me that my friend would ask me to preach that morning. When I found the pastor's study, my pastor friend was looking through a book. With book in hand, he looked up, greeted me, and asked me if I would like to preach. I already had decided upon a sermon—but he didn't know it! As I sat on the platform and watched the people, I noted that no one in the crowd was smiling, except for one young woman on my right. When the pastor recognized visitors, to my surprise, the woman with a smile raised her hand to acknowledge that she was a visitor. It dawned on me that the church must have a spirit of discouragement. During the sermon I spoke briefly about discouragement and how to deal with it in a spiritual way. Some members came forward during the invitation and acknowledged that they had been discouraged. Even a group of people, like a church, can be affected by this deadly spiritual sickness.

## The Resolution of Discouragement

ON THAT SPRING DAY during my quiet time, as I read Romans 12:11, "Never be lacking in zeal, but keep your spiritual fervor, serving the Lord," it began to occur to me that discouragement may not just be human weakness—it may be sin. I learned during my high school days how to deal with sin. We confess it, and God forgives. The problem had been that no one had told me that discouragement was sin. The fact is that it may be one of the most common sins of committed Christians.

Actually I should have known years earlier that discouragement is sin, because God says not to do it. If I do anything He says not to do, it is disobedience—thus it is sin. In fact, as I began to look for this truth in the Bible, I found four or five ways the Bible warns us not to get discouraged. In Luke 18:1 we are told, "Then Jesus told his disciples a parable to show that they should always pray and not give up." The word translated "give up" also implies discouragement. When a Christian finally throws in the towel and gives up on God, he is discouraged.

In Galatians 6:9, Paul said, "Let us not become weary in doing good, for at the proper time we will reap a harvest if we do not give up." To become weary is a similar idea to discouragement. It does not mean we should never get tired physically or even tired of constant Christian activity. Instead, we are commanded never to become weary with reference to serving and loving God. If we do, we have become discouraged.

Again in Hebrews 12:3 the believer is told not to "lose heart." In the KJV, 2 Corinthians 4:1 says that we should not "faint." Both of these are also similar ideas to becoming discouraged. Then, in Joshua 1:9, the Lord told Joshua (and us) not to get discouraged. These five ways should have been sufficient for me to see the problem—God commands us not to get discouraged. As a teenager I was taught if I disobeyed God, it was sin—whether it was deliberate and malicious sin or the sin of omission.

As I have thought about it over the years, I have thought of at least three reasons why it is sin to be discouraged. First, God says not to do it. Second, it is self-pity to be discouraged, and any time we wallow in self-pity, it surely is sinful. Third, discouragement is a lack of faith, as Romans 14:23 says, "And everything that does not come from faith is sin." It became pretty clear to me. Here was a super-common problem for the committed Christian, and I have never read that discouragement is sin! Perhaps many Christians would be more powerful in their walk with God if they only knew how to deal with this common sin.

With the understanding that discouragement is sinful we have a solution to the problem. If you really are a committed believer, Jesus Christ is your Lord, and you feel you have given up, there may be a simple solution. This problem may have plagued you for months or even years, but it can be broken, and you can have the joy of the Lord again. I am so certain this is from God. It has worked over and over in my life. I have shared it with many others, and it has worked for them. Many of them have been pastors and Christian workers. In fact, I think discouragement may be the biggest problem pastors face—and the only way it can be solved is in their personal walk with Jesus.

The first step to break the power of discouragement over you is to recognize that you really are discouraged. Be sure it is not a bad day, a low-energy level, or a simple seasonal period of the blahs. Second, you must admit that you have allowed discouragement to become sin, and you must confess it as sin to God. Then you should make a fresh surrender of your heart to Jesus as your Lord. Ask the Holy Spirit, who is in you, to take full control again. You have not lost Him; He has simply yielded control because of your sin. Fourth, rejoice (Phil. 4:4) that He is in control of your life again—regardless of how you feel.

Perhaps the emotional baggage of a time of discouragement will go away slowly. Sometimes the "cloud" which follows us during discouragement goes away instantly, and sometimes it is a few days before we feel joyful again. Remember that emotions are not in charge of your life—Jesus is! But, if the struggle you have had has been discouragement, it will leave if you follow this biblical plan. God always forgives us of our sins, and He breaks the power of sin over us when we confess and forsake it (1 John 1:9).

Several years ago, when my daughter Meredith was about six, our family went to the Mid-South fair in Memphis. Meredith has always loved all kinds of animals, so she insisted that we go in one of the animal buildings. This particular one had several cages with incubators of hatched and un-hatched chicks. I was looking at one cage where only one of the baby chicks had been hatched. As the chick walked around with its new-found freedom, a thought hit me. Discouragement is like an egg shell. In the egg it is gloomy, dark, and it surrounds the poor chick. After about 21 days, God has built into the chick the desire to get out of the egg. He also has equipped the baby chick with the equipment to get free. On the end of the chick's beak is a hard substance called an "egg tooth." The chick can peck on the egg shell, and before long the egg tooth creates a crack in the shell. Light then beams into the egg. I have imagined what the chick is thinking about now, "I'm here in this dark and gloomy shell, and there is light and room to roam out there. I think I'll change locations!" Then the chick pushes with its head or feet or wing, and bursts from the shell—and out comes the chick! It is now free and away from the dark, gloomy life of the shell.

I'm sure you see the application to the problem of discouragement. We often—even as committed, sold-out Christians—exist in a dark, gloomy world of discouragement. There seems to be no logical way out but to try harder for God—and then it often just gets darker and gloomier. But, Jesus Christ, our deliverer, has given us a "spiritual egg tooth," just like He equipped the little chick for survival. If we will face the mountain of gloom which is before, behind, and around us, and if we will deal with discouragement God's way—we can be set free.

I heard somebody say that during WWII Winston Churchill once told a group, "Never give up! Never, never give up! Never, never, never give up!" I agree with Churchill. Jerry Falwell once said that the measure of a great person of God was what it takes to discourage them. However, I am frail, and I have given up. I am glad to say that I'm learning to shorten my periods of discouragement from months to hours. I believe you can too!

# 2

# DOUBT

## *Does It Ever End*?

I BECAME A CHRISTIAN when I was 16 and a tenth grader in High School. The main reason I gave my life to Jesus was because of a guy in my speech class named Howard Lamb. He just glowed with the joy of Jesus The first speech I remember Howard giving in our class, he put a map of India behind the podium and looked at us, his peers, and said, "God has called me to be a missionary to India." I was astounded! As far as I can recall, I had never heard a student talk openly about God or Jesus unless they were invited to by a teacher or some school authority. And here, early in my first year of high school I encountered Howard joyfully talking about Jesus. I just couldn't get away from him and his joy. About 4 or 5 months after I met Howard, he brought an old 33 vinyl album to school. It was simply a man preaching about Jesus and telling funny stories. His name was Bob Harrington, and I later knew him as the Chaplain of Bourbon Street. About this time I surrendered all I was to Jesus and was wonderfully born again. The day I gave my life to Jesus, I stopped cursing and my attitudes began to change, especially towards girls. My friends even began to change. I was really, "on fire for God."

In less than a year, I went through a very difficult time, and I got depressed. It lasted a few months, and during that time I struggled painfully about my salvation. I had only been saved a year, yet I doubted that I had really given my life to Jesus. I woke up almost every morning with doubts on my mind. They were with me all day long. I just didn't know what to do about it. Things got so bad that my stepfather invited a preacher friend of his over to the house to talk to me about my problems. Within a few minutes of his arrival, I was weeping and baring my heart to him in front of both my parents. Very soon I was on my knees praying again to receive Jesus into my life. Now I'm certain that I was already saved, but here I was giving my life to Jesus again, not sure that I had been saved the first time. I kept serving the Lord, and when the depression lifted, I was able to joyfully testify about Jesus again. It was a harrowing experience and one that I really didn't expect to encounter after I had been saved.

Later I discovered that this experience was very common among genuine believers. I'm talking about the experience of doubting one's salvation. I was a youth director in 3 churches, and of course, I had the privilege of speaking to many young people about their relationship with the Lord. In doing this, I discovered that many teenagers go through the experience of doubting their salvation. In Arkansas a teenager named Danny came to me more than once with his bushy hair and outgoing personality. He still could not get satisfied that he was a genuine Christian. Of course I didn't know if he was saved or not, so I tried to share with him from the Bible and from my heart the best way I knew how. Finally he seemed to be settled that he had really given his life to Jesus.

One year during my graduate work in seminary, 7 students professed to have been saved since they came to the seminary. Quite honestly I was skeptical, and I guessed that some of them had already been saved and were just receiving assurance. But I really didn't know for sure what was happening. I would always prefer to have seminary students and ministers after they graduate who have really been saved than those who are still doubting their salvation and are unsaved!

One of the most devastating spiritual problems that committed Christians have is this matter of doubting their salvation. Doubts seem to paralyze Christians from sharing their faith, from being bold and serving Jesus, and even from enjoying a rich devotional life. Doubting is simply horrible!

## The Bible on Doubting

THE BIBLE HAS a good bit to say in this area about the problem of doubting your salvation. Jude 23 says "Be merciful to those who doubt." No wonder Jude told us to be merciful to doubters, because doubt is a problem that is as all consuming as grief, and most of us are aware what the loss of a loved one can do to our perspective. It is easy to think of Thomas when we consider doubts; of course he is known as "doubting Thomas." We are not sure what Thomas doubted. We know he doubted the resurrection of Christ, and we are certain that he was doubtful at other times during Christ's ministry. We are really not certain that he doubted his own personal salvation, but it only makes sense that someone who even doubts the resurrection of Christ would have a hard time getting on solid ground about his personal salvation. Romans 8:16 tells us that the Spirit bears witness with our spirit (in other words He tells us inside that we are children of God). When we are not walking in the power of the Spirit, it is natural to begin to wonder if we even belong to the Spirit, and when we really get backslidden from God, doubts are very common.

God wants us to know for certain that we are saved. What a cruel God we would have if He asked us to wait until we die to know for certain if we are going to heaven or not. Jesus is not cruel. He wants us to be at peace with our salvation.

Since the 1980s a few Baptist preachers have become rather well known by the number of professions of faith which are made by church members during their meetings. These men seem to have good motives, and they really love Jesus and the souls of men. They go into churches for revival meetings or evangelistic crusades, and they preach that you must know you're saved at all times, and if you do not know this, then you're not saved. I have heard one of these men quoted as saying, "If you're 99% sure you are saved, then you're 100% lost." People who hear this message are stirred deeply. Everyone wants to go to heaven. We may or may not care about others going to heaven, but we certainly want to go. These well meaning ministers often cause great confusion in some of the churches they leave, because people begin to sort out if they were already saved or not before their spiritual experience during the campaign. A man who works with me at our seminary recently said that he wrestled over his salvation for 2 years after one of these evangelists left his church in Memphis.

One of my colleagues wrote an article on "Martinism." This doctrinal teaching occurred in Baptist life at the beginning of the 20th century. A preacher named Martin began to preach that those who have doubts about their salvation are probably lost. He achieved some renown especially in Texas and Mississippi, but he also caused much confusion. B. H. Carroll, the founder of Southwestern Baptist Seminary in Forth Worth, Texas, felt so strongly about what he was doing that he led his church to disfellowship Martin. It is really serious when believers begin doubting their salvation.

I know that sincere Christians can doubt their salvation—I have done it myself, and I consider myself to be a sincere Christian. In my seminary teaching I realized that this was a big problem. To illustrate how big a problem it was, in some courses, I have asked my students, "How many of you have seriously doubted your salvation since you are certain you were saved?" Usually about 75 to 80% of the students will raise their hands and sometimes it's been 100% of the class. Now these are committed Christians. They love Jesus and they are sacrificing to be at seminary. Seminary students are probably 25 to 28 years old on the average. Most of them are married, and many of them have children. They work hard to provide for the needs of their families as well as working in the church and going to seminary. These sincere Christians have had serious doubts about their salvation. If you have had doubts, then you are not alone. I know that doesn't relieve your doubts, but it lets you know the company that you're in.

## The Reasons We Doubt Our Salvation

KNOWING JESUS CHRIST in a personal way is life's greatest experience. When we live for Jesus day by day, we experience life's greatest joy—abundant life in Christ (John 10:10). We also are assured of Heaven. In John 14, Jesus promised that He was going to heaven, preparing a place for us, and coming back to get us. Nothing in life can substitute for these promises; however, committed Christians can and will sometimes have serious doubts about their salvation. What causes this? Here are 5 major reasons why Christians doubt their salvation:

1. Sin in Our Lives—When Christians have sin in their lives and allow it to stay there un-confessed, a barrier develops between them and God. If we allow this barrier to remain, it sometimes will cause us to doubt our salvation. After living for Jesus for 2 1/2 years in high school, I graduated and headed toward college in 1969. These were crazy years! The Vietnam War was in full swing, and the hippie movement was going on. People were dying, rebelling against authority, and the Jesus movement was raging among young people. It was an exciting time to be alive for Christians.

My first year of college, I decided to pledge a fraternity, and I slowly began to drift away from the Lord. I was also in love for the first time with the love of my life—my wife Carol. As I got further and further away from the Lord that first year of college, I came to the place that I just could not talk to God and read my Bible—I just could not do it. There was such a barrier between me and God that I was immobilized spiritually. I do not remember doubting my salvation at this time, but it was a perfect setup for me to do so. When these events happen in the lives of believers, many begin to doubt their salvation.

Sin in your life left un-confessed for a period of time may cause you to doubt your salvation. What should you do about this? It's pretty obvious you should confess your sins and repent of them, turning away from evil. This is maybe the most obvious and common reason that people doubt their salvation.

2. Wrong Doctrine—When Carol and I began dating late in our high school years, I shared with her how great my relationship with Jesus was and that I was sure of my salvation. She shared with me how she was not sure of her salvation. She went to a church that did not teach assurance of salvation. She went through a confirmation class when she was ten or eleven, she was taught some important doctrines, and then she was "taken into the church." At this point the church assumed that she and the others of the group were saved; however Carol was not saved. During her teenage years, she told me that she would lie in bed in the dark and wonder if she died, would she go to heaven. At that point she would not have gone to heaven, but God is gracious; He worked in her heart, and she gave her life to Jesus after we were married.

Many Christian groups teach that you cannot know for certain that you are going to heaven. They use the same Bible that we use, but they interpret some important passages differently than we do. Some of those important passages are John 10:28 where Jesus says that we are placed in His hand and no one can take us out of His hand. Romans 8:38-39 clearly says that nothing can take us away from the love of God. I have heard the argument that nothing can, but you can deny the Lord and lose your salvation. However, this passage in Romans states clearly that no one can remove us from the love of God. It just so happens that you and I are someone, and we even cannot remove ourselves from the hand of God. Hebrews 13:5 simply says that God will never leave us. In John 5:24, Jesus Christ clearly says that when you have believed in Jesus, you already have eternal life. These passages are just a few of those which teach that once we're in the hand of God we cannot be removed—salvation cannot be taken away from us. Wrong doctrine, however, can make us doubt that we are saved.

3. Our Baptism Is Out of Order—Just two weeks ago at the church we attend, one of my friends from my Sunday school class was baptized. He is in his 50's, he has been a solid Christian, so I wondered why he was baptized. I asked him this, and he said that he realized that he was saved after he was baptized the first time. This is a common story of many people. I went through it myself as have many other believers. I was saved, as I mentioned earlier, when I was in high school, but I was baptized when I was 11. I never received baptism after I was really saved. I just could not settle the question until I was in my late 30's. I was teaching at the seminary, and one spring I was terribly disturbed about matters in my heart, and I promised the Lord that I would get my baptism straight. I did, and when I was baptized correctly (that is after my salvation) this matter of doubt was settled for me.

4. A Difficult Background—Don't ever let anybody tell you that Christians will not have huge and difficult problems. It is just not true. Believers have the presence of the Holy Spirit, the grace of God, and countless other benefits as a result of giving our lives to Jesus; however, we still go through big problems. If you are not sure about it, just examine the life of Jesus and the life of Paul. Problems seem to pop up at every turn for the Lord. Paul experienced difficulties beyond what anybody would imagine—shipwrecks, stoning, rejection, mobs against him, and so on. I know that you have personally experienced problems already, no matter your age. You have been rejected by people that you thought loved you, you have been hurt deeply by people that you know love you, you have experienced physical difficulties, tragedies, and more. If you have a particularly difficult background and you experienced much of the hurt of your life before you were grown, you are probably more apt to doubt your salvation. A tough background leads some people to doubt almost everything, and their relationship with Jesus is one of the important things in their lives that they doubt.

This is really a tough matter to discuss. I don't know of any Scripture that ties the connection between difficulties in youth and doubting our salvation. I simply know that I experienced this and others have, too. My father died when I was 5, and I was left alone with my mother. By the time I was 6, all of my grandparents were dead. My mother remarried, and my mother and stepfather loved each other but had a very difficult marriage that wound up in divorce when I was 18. They argued and fought for about 3 years before the divorce. These factors and others led to a rather difficult upbringing and seemed to contribute to the doubts I had about my salvation.

If you have a particularly difficult background, you may struggle with resentment or with bitterness toward God. You may also struggle with bitterness toward those who contributed to your problems. These problems, along with your other problems, may have brought confusion and doubts to your life. These doubts may have led you to have a hard time believing that God would save you. You can believe God's truth rather than the lies of your past; He loves you and wants you to know it.

5. You May Not Be a Christian and Think You Are—Some people who are active in church and grow up in committed Christian homes make early or confused decisions to give their lives to Jesus, and they actually were not converted. I have heard people say that the devil could make us doubt our salvation, but I cannot imagine our enemy encouraging us to be truly saved when we are not. Does that mean that all doubts prove that we're lost? Absolutely not, but some people think they are saved when they are actually lost.

I mentioned my wife Carol earlier. During our sophomore year in college, God moved in my life in a wonderful way, and I gave my life back to Jesus totally. Then He very quickly confirmed that he wanted me in the ministry. This caused confusion in Carol, and it made her doubt her own relationship with the Lord. One night we were sitting in my car on the campus of the University of Alabama, and she shared these doubts with me. I showed her how she could very simply give her life to Christ and pray to let Jesus come into her heart. She did pray to receive Jesus, and we thought she was saved. At that time I did not understand that she must surrender to Jesus to be truly saved, so I didn't tell her that. Later, after much confusion about her spiritual condition, Carol did surrender her life to Jesus, and she was saved my last year of seminary. She had doubted her salvation at several times during her life, because she was not a Christian. God graciously pursued her until she did surrender to Him.

This could be the situation that you are experiencing, or that someone you love has gone through. They simply need to surrender their life to Jesus Christ. Don't be confused as we were by the idea of simply asking Jesus into your heart. The Bible says in Romans 10:19, "If you confess Jesus as Lord and believe in your heart that God has raised him from the dead, you will be saved." The Bible makes it very clear that we must surrender to the Lord Jesus. If you haven't done so your doubts will not be settled.

What does it take to be saved? It is not difficult, it is not confusing, and it's very simple. First, you must acknowledge that you need the Lord Jesus, and that you cannot save yourself on your own. He died on the cross for your sins and rose from the grave for your salvation. Then you must come face to face with the fact that you are a sinner— you have disobeyed and rebelled against God (Romans 3:23). Having done this you must repent of your sins. To repent means to ask God to forgive you and to allow Him to change you so that you can turn and do what He wishes for you to do. Next, on a particular day and a particular moment, we must choose to surrender our lives to Jesus and allow Him to be Lord of our life. How do you do this? Ask Him. Ask Him to come live in your life, to forgive your sins, and to be the Lord and master of your life.

Doubting your salvation can be one of the most difficult experiences of your life. But God has a solution; He wants to help you. He loves you, He made you fearfully and wonderfully, and you are very special to Him. Don't drop this matter until it is resolved. If you desire to grow spiritually as a committed Christian, you must settle the matter of your own salvation. It is worth any price you may pay. Seek out somebody who loves Jesus, tell them you're situation, and ask for their help. You can get past your doubts.

# 3

# RELATIONSHIPS

## *The Broken and the Healing*

THE MOST FAMOUS FEUD that I know about in all of American history is the bloody feud between the Hatfield's and the McCoy's in Kentucky and West Virginia. One family lived on one side of the Tug Fork River and the other family lived on the other. Of course, the feud lasted for decades in the 1800s. It appears that the conflict began over a pig. One person was offended at the other, and the other became offended at the first, and soon the bad relationship began to spread through the extended family on both sides. Some shots rang out, a "killing" occurred, and the war was on. Before the feud was settled, nine people had died. I'll bet that some of the people involved were Christians. On a website regarding this famous family war, there was a recent picture of a joint family reunion of the Hatfield's and McCoy's. They apparently love one another now and get along as Forrest Gump would say, "Like peas and carrots."

As a young believer, all I knew to do when I had a bad relationship with someone was to say, "I'm sorry." As I have learned more about the biblical teaching on this subject and as I have practiced it many times now, I realize that what I learned as a teenager wasn't a very bad approach.

In the eleventh grade, I rode to school with my best friend Robin. He had a late 30's or early 40's coupe which he had customized. The seats were rolled and pleated, and they were light blue. One day after school we stopped at Hardy's a fast food restaurant, and I bought a milk shake. It was so thick that I could turn it over and it wouldn't come out. So I said to Robin, "Look, I can turn this milk shake over, and it won't come out." About the time I said that, it plopped out on his beautiful car, and boy, was he miffed! At that time all I knew to do was to say, "Robin, I'm sorry, Robin, I am sorry." I said it over and over. I learned that there was clear biblical teaching and practical advice for Christians on this very subject.

My first staff position in a local church was at the First Baptist Church of West Point, Mississippi. I served there twice; once before I was out of college, and once right after I graduated from college at the University of Alabama. It was a great gig. After college, I was assistant pastor, educational director, in charge of outreach, and I led the children's worship services. I loved my job. It was exciting, and we were reaching a lot of people for Jesus. I was enthusiastic to the point of being rambunctious, so I wound up offending some people. I learned that (now that I was in the ministry) it was a little harder to get forgiveness when I offended folks. There is always this idea that preachers are not going to do bad things, when in fact often we do about as many as anybody else.

After that experience, I headed to seminary in Little Rock, Arkansas. In my second year, the seminary moved to Memphis, and I attended a Christian seminar taught by Bill Gothard. It was at this seminar that I first heard how to seek forgiveness from people properly. What I had been doing was not bad, it just was not complete. I made a commitment at that seminar to get right with everyone that God showed me I needed to talk with. My list was only 3 people deep, but doing it was difficult.

The first person I called was the pastor I worked with in West Point. He was so gracious to me! I told him that I felt as though I had left the church without our relationship being what it should be, and I wanted him to forgive me. Would he forgive me? That's the angle I had learned. By the time I asked him these questions, tears were falling from my eyes. I was not really weeping, I was just "tearing." The pastor said, "Certainly I will forgive you," and, "Now I think even more of you spiritually than I did before." I talked to the other people on my list and received forgiveness from them also. So I was on the road to learning how to gain forgiveness and a clear conscience.

A clear conscience can be simply defined, "I don't know of anyone that I have offended whom I have not asked for their forgiveness and sincerely tried to get right with them. I also know of no one who has offended me against whom I'm holding a grudge."

I'd like to pause in this narrative and ask you, according to the above, do you have a clear conscience right now? Paul said to Timothy, "I strive always to maintain a clear conscience toward God and man." Acts 24:16. Jesus said in Matthew 5:23-24 (a part of the Sermon on the Mount), "Therefore if you are offering your gift at the altar and there remember that your brother has something against you, leave your gift there in front of the altar. First go and be reconciled to your brother; then come and offer your gift."

My New Testament Survey professor in seminary said the key word in the Matthew 5 passage is, "remember." We do not have to worry about relationships that are broken if we don't remember them. God will bring them back to our memory if He wishes to. We do have to be concerned about the broken relationships that we remember. Usually it's not very hard to remember the broken relationships in our lives. Jesus says in this passage that it is more important for us to be reconciled to people than it is to offer our gifts at the altar. Since New Testament Christians no longer offer gifts at the altar, other than our tithes and offerings, I have always thought it was fair to equate this statement of the Lord's with the time we spend with

Him. When we are offering our heart to Him in our devotional time, and remember that someone has something against us, that's the time to go and get right with people.

It is important to say this correctly, (I have wronged you in what I did or what I said, and I have come to you to ask you this question, Will you forgive me?). Then we are to wait for an answer, to see what they tell us. If they are not forthright in telling us they forgive us, this is certainly not a time to argue or debate, it's a time to humble ourselves and listen. On the other hand, the Lord Jesus said in Matthew 18:15, "If your brother sins against you, go and show him his fault, just between the two of you." In this situation Jesus is not teaching us to reconcile with our brother when we have offended him; He is telling us we should be reconciled when our brother has offended us. Someone has said truthfully that offended Christians should meet one another in the middle on the way to get right with each other.

Once I had a rift with another professor where I teach. About the time I got to my office, I felt terrible so I went back to his office and told him how sorry I was. He said to me, "I was about to come to talk to you about this." I wish I could say that this is always what happens in my relationships that are broken, but it is not. It is the ideal though.

One of my favorite Old Testament stories concerns Jacob and Esau in Genesis 32 and 33. Jacob was the sly one who had wronged Esau more than once. The crowning blow of the offence to his brother was when he took his birthright. For years after this, the brothers were separated as Jacob spent many years earning the right to marry Rachael. Esau had been gaining power all the while, and had a small army at his disposal. When Jacob came back to the land of his fathers, Esau came to meet him. Of course Jacob was disturbed at the thought since Esau was the rough one of the brothers, and since Jacob had so deeply offended Esau. The night before their meeting was the night when Jacob wrestled with an angel (the Lord Jesus Himself), and Jacob had his name changed to Israel. The next morning Jacob looked up and he saw Esau coming with his 400 men. He was desperately afraid, and divided his family hoping that at least one of the groups would survive Esau's army. However when Esau saw Jacob, he ran to meet him and embraced him. "He threw his arms around his neck and kissed him and they wept." Genesis 33:4. Jacob found forgiveness without even a word. His method of confrontation to receive forgiveness was simply to show up and to be humble. He bowed several times before Esau before they embraced.

This story is such a great picture of New Testament reconciliation. It is not a complicated thing, it is, however, something that many committed Christians simply refuse to do.

I have imagined what might have taken place the night before the Lord's crucifixion. Simon Peter was weeping as he walked down a back alley of Jerusalem, and I imagine that he ran face to face into Judas Iscariot. Of course Simon was a rowdy sort, and he could have pulled his sword out. This time he probably would not have missed. But somehow in my heart, I don't believe that is what he would have done. Simon had repented, and he had been forgiven. For imagination's sake can we imagine what it would have been like if Simon had looked with love at Judas. And He spoke some kind words to him. Then Peter threw his arms around him, and said, "Brother, I don't like what you have done, I cannot believe that you did this, but I would like to be the first to tell you that I forgive you." We cannot rewrite history, and God in His Word has already told us what the fate of Judas would be. But can you imagine, humanly speaking, what might have taken place in the heart of Judas? Would he have wept, would he have sought forgiveness like Peter had? This is only speculation, but forgiveness is just that powerful, and it often will not happen unless we ask people to forgive us, or tell them that we forgive them.

It is really curious why we wait to ask forgiveness or grant forgiveness, since it hurts so much to have a broken relationship with someone whom we love. It may be one of the worst forms of spiritual pain. Sometimes it's all absorbing and always on our mind. I had a problem with a fellow seventh grader, and he suggested that we should put on the boxing gloves and fight the next day. I will never forget the agony I went through worrying about that broken relationship and the potential fight. I couldn't sleep. I talked with my mother over, and over. The next day I went to school, and he never mentioned the fight. Somehow our relationship was just fine after that, but many relationships are not reconciled that easily.

I learned at a Christian seminar during seminary that we should seek forgiveness from someone if we have wronged them—even if we are only five or ten percent at fault. It seemed like a good rule of thumb to me. So that's what I practiced for awhile. Then while I was a pastor, I was at a youth camp in Arkansas with about 20 young people from my church. I do not think I have ever seen a bunch of young people with such a bad attitude. It was a nice camp, there were other churches there, and we were away from home for almost a week. The bad attitude settled in, and 2 of my oldest boys were involved. One of them I will call Tom. He puffed up like a bullfrog, and he pouted and complained about camp over and over.

We started on Monday, so by Tuesday evening I had really had my fill. I was one of the leaders of the camp, and my young people were causing the most trouble. Before bedtime we had the snack shack open, and we were getting snacks. Now remember I was Tom's pastor, and he was taught to respect authority in his home. I said to him very forthrightly, "Tom, you have acted like a baby, your attitude stinks, and you've affected other people, God is not happy with this." Tom was hurt, but I went away from the encounter knowing that I had done the right thing. I told him the truth, I hadn't screamed at him, so I felt good about it.

The next morning during our Bible study, we studied about conditions for prayer. While the teacher was talking about relationships being correct as a condition during prayer, the Holy Spirit seemed to say to me, you need to go to Tom and get right. I was arguing in my heart (and maybe with the Lord) that I had done right and I didn't need to get right with Tom. Sitting on that bench, God taught me a wonderful lesson. If someone is hurt at you and it is not your fault at all, not five or ten percent, but they're still hurt at you, you still need to go to them to get right. So I obeyed God right after the Bible study. Walking on a trail by a lake I said, "Tom, let me talk to you." He came over with a good attitude, and I apologized to him for hurting him. He said, "Ah, Brother Steve that's okay." We parted with our relationship restored. By this time I had been pastor of this church for about 3 years, and I saw God work in the hearts of our teenagers more than I had seen since I had been the pastor of the church. I wondered if the confrontation with Tom and our reconciliation had a lot to do with that. I really believe it did. God wants His children to dwell together in harmony.

I was speaking at a church on the subject of a clear conscience and getting right with those we have offended. The pastor of the church stated at the end of the service that as far as he knew, he had a clear conscience and was right with everyone in the church. A young woman was sitting on about the 3rd or 4th pew, and she had a very hurt look on her face. The pastor remembered that he had been harsh with the father of the young woman. So during the revival meeting, Pastor Jimmy went to see the man and got the relationship right between the two of them. Sometimes it takes another person to remind us that we do not have a good relationship with someone.

Matthew 18 has been discussed, debated, analyzed, denied, and at times practiced in recent years. It is a very important passage concerning reconciliation and broken relationships. Jesus clearly gives three steps to practice when relationships are broken. I have only known a few churches that openly practice what Jesus teaches in Matthew 18. The key text is Matthew 18:15-17. These three verses are vital. The Lord tells us to go to someone who has sinned against us—go alone. If the problem is not resolved, then He says to go and take one or two people along. Finally He says we are to take the matter to the church. If he refuses to listen to what the church says, we are to treat this person as a pagan or tax collector.

I have studied this verse, discussed it for hours, and tried to practice it in my ministry. Several sideline truths have been made clear to me. First, Jesus never said that we had to take steps one, two, and three quickly. In fact, I encourage people to do them slowly because human emotions rise quickly and subside slowly. Give the offending person some time to deal with his offense. Second, Jesus never said it was wrong to go to the offending party more than once in private or at the second step before we go on to the next step. You may feel led by the Lord to go back a second time individually. Third, I would encourage you not to vote on this matter in your church, if your church is the kind that votes on issues. Jesus does not tell us in this text to vote; He simply says to tell it to the church. Fourth, I would let the deacons or the pastor lead during this fragile time, and let them determine when to tell the matter to the church and what to say. Fifth, the Lord said in verse 17 to treat the person as a pagan or tax collector. The church is not to treat pagans and tax collector harshly or in a mean way. We are to love them, we are to encourage them to be saved, and we are to invite them to our church. When a person has allowed a situation to go to step three, we are aware that this person is not a Christian. Jesus is saying they are not a Christian and to treat them as such.

In my own Christian walk, I have only had to go to step two—taking someone with me. Here is what I have learned about reconciliation that is so important if we will go to those we have offended (or to those who have offended us) in love, humility, and meekness: most broken relationships can be reconciled at step one.

## Family

THIS TEACHING OF JESUS doesn't just apply to church members; it also applies to family members. In fact, if you are married you will probably seek the forgiveness of your marriage partner many more times than you will anyone else. This has certainly been true in my marriage. Carol and I are different. We have different tastes, outlooks, spiritual gifts, and backgrounds. We do and say things differently, and we have had the wonderful privilege of saying I'm sorry many, many times. I am the extrovert and the loud one. In Colossians 3:19 we are told, "Husbands, love your wives and do not be harsh with them." I remember clearly when the Holy Spirit prompted me and seemed to say to me that this teaching applies to everyone, not just wives.

We are not to be harsh with anybody. An African-American pastor friend of mine taught me this principle by saying, "Steve, be diplomatic with your people. Jesus was never harsh one on one with anybody." I was stunned when that idea hit me, and I realized that I should not be harsh with anybody. When we are harsh with our spouse, we have grieved the Holy Spirit, and we need to get right with God and with them.

## Conclusion

I HAVE BEEN TROUBLED in the last few years as I have observed a practice in the lives of some Christian leaders. Some have chosen not to get right with those they have offended or those who have offended them. They have simply "blown it off" and handled the relationship by staying away from the other Christian. This attitude is totally unacceptable to God and contrary to His teaching. God expects us to obey in these matters and to get right with those that we have hurt or who have hurt us. Committed Christians must learn to practice deference. Deference is simply choosing not to do or say what bothers or offends someone else. It is learning the preferences of those that we love, and choosing to do what they want, not what we want. If we do choose to mend broken relationships the biblical way, we will enjoy fellowship with those who have previously been precious to us. We will also enjoy the fellowship of our Heavenly Father. We will build up the kingdom of God, and we may even sleep better. If we choose not to be involved in mending broken relationships, it will hurt our fellowship with other people, with Jesus Christ, and we will probably fret, worry, and lose sleep over the broken relationships.

My mother and I have kept a good relationship just about all of my life. We've worked at it, we have forgiven each other, and we've brought things up that we needed to talk about. She is so special to me. I can't imagine having a broken relationship with her. Let's not allow that to happen with anybody we love.

# 4

# BITTERNESS

## *Bitter or Better?*

CAN A COMMITTED CHRISTIAN get resentful and bitter? Of course we can! Everybody gets bitter probably several times during their life time. All it takes for us to be bitter is to be hurt and then not deal with the hurt properly with the Lord. In other words my wife can speak very negatively or sharply at me and I can have my feelings hurt. Normally I am able to go away, and before too long I'm able to forgive her. But let's imagine that I do not forgive her, and I hang on to this hurt. I am wounded, things are not good in my heart, and they are not right in my marriage. I decide to hang on to this hurt, and I hang on for weeks and then months, constantly remembering the way she spoke to me. Over time the bitterness begins to grow and it gets bigger and bigger as I mull it over in my heart. Before long there is a root of bitterness (Hebrews 12:13). That root of bitterness goes down into my soul and makes me much more susceptible to other hurt and bitterness, and it ruins my walk with God. I am now the product and the captive of bitterness. Bitterness has hurt my relationship with God, my relationship with my wife, and as a result it has hurt other relationships and other areas of my life.

I heard the story of a young man who was about to be promoted to the office of Vice President of his corporation. He told his wife about the situation with great pride over and over. She almost didn't like to be around him because of his cockiness.

The big day arrived and he was actually promoted to the office of vice president. He came home, and opened the door to his house. His wife had looked out the door and could tell by the way he was strutting that he had been promoted. He walked in the door and exclaimed, "Hello, is anybody home?" His wife came into the foyer of the house and he was standing there with a huge smile on his face and said, "Well they finally saw the light and promoted me to be Vice President!" His wife snarled at him and said to him rather quickly, "Vice President, why Vice Presidents are a dime a dozen. Down at the supermarket where I shop they have a Vice President in charge of prunes!"

Well, this hurt his feelings, and he could not get over the pain that his wife would not support him and that she would even make fun of him. So the next day he went to work and entered his new office with his new secretary and a new plaque that said "Vice President." He sat at his Vice Presidential desk for hours unable to do anything, except mull over what his wife had said about prunes. Finally he reached for the phone book and looked up the supermarket where his wife shopped. He called the number and said rather sheepishly to the operator, "Excuse me ma'am but could I please speak to the Vice President in charge of prunes?" He waited expecting to hear a laugh, and instead she retorted, "Would that be the Vice President in charge of packaged or bulk prunes?"

Our husband in this scene could be extremely hurt over this interchange, especially when he heard that they actually had a Vice President or two over prunes. Something as silly as this could cause bitterness, resentment, and genuine marriage problems.

Many have said for years that the number one cause of divorce and problems in marriages is due to money issues. I have never believed that, and I still do not. I believe that the main cause of marital disharmony and divorce is hurt, resentment, and bitterness.

The Bible is rather plain when it speaks about bitterness. Many stories in Scripture illustrate people who were bitter or could have been bitter. For instance could Adam have been bitter at Eve when Eve choose to rebel against God? Sure.

Was Cain bitter at Abel? It appears he was because Abel had pleased God with his offering of blood. Then Cain killed his brother—a sure sign of bitterness.

Was Joseph bitter at his brothers or were his brothers bitter at Joseph? From all I can see in the text, it does not look like Joseph was bitter at his brothers, but it certainly appears that his brothers were bitter at Joseph for his cocky or arrogant attitude.

Was Saul bitter at David? It appears that Saul genuinely was bitter at David because of his jealously which raged inside of him for years.

Was Jeremiah bitter at God? I'm not sure. Someone has said that all bitterness is ultimately bitterness at God. I am not sure about that, but I do know that much bitterness is toward God.

Were the nine disciples who were not allowed to be in the inner circle with Jesus, Peter, James, and John bitter? We know they were jealous. They showed signs of true jealously as they questioned one another late in the ministry of Jesus. Peter, James, and John came down from the mountain of transfiguration describing the wonders of seeing Jesus as He really is; the other nine disciples had missed seeing Elijah and Moses. How would we have felt?

Was Paul bitter at the leaders at Lystra? They loved him, tried to worship him and then stoned him, leaving him for dead. I think I would have been bitter. Apparently he was not. He went right back to Lystra after being stoned. We know he had to be hurt, physically and emotionally. These people had turned on him.

Yes bitterness is everywhere. It is in the Bible, it is in our lives, and it sometimes seems to be all around us.

I spoke at a church in Hot Springs, Arkansas in the 1990's. After I spoke, a gentleman of 80 years of age came up to me and said, "You are having lunch with me. I told him I would have to check with my wife—he already had talked to her. He told me that we would ride with him. I told him I would drive—he was pushy to say the least.

My wife and I met this man, and his wife at a restaurant. We had a pleasant meal. He was a dentist and still practicing. He said that he had treated the families of both United States Senators in Arkansas, and I was quite impressed. Then I began to understand why he wanted to have lunch with me. He asked me, "How do you know so much about bitterness?" I had just spoken on bitterness at the church he attended. I told him, "I've been bitter myself and I had to deal with it. I have helped other people do the same, and I have studied the Bible on bitterness." As we talked he began to reveal his real question. He and his son had been estranged for years, and there was bitterness in their relationship. He was hurting over this situation, and he wanted relief. He wanted to know how to deal with his and his son's bitterness. We tried to help.

## The Burden of Bitterness

BITTERNESS IS SUCH a heavy burden that for some people it is almost indescribable. It can cause physical ailments. Bitterness may aggravate high blood pressure, and may possibly lead to heart disease; bitterness probably can make mental illness worse and perhaps even bring on some latent forms of mental illness. Dr. I. McMillan in his book *None of These Diseases* discusses the many physical problems bitterness can cause or aggravate.

Bitterness can harm relationships. It can cause deep marital problems—in fact bitterness can lead to divorce and has done so many times. Bitterness can even lead to divorce in Christian homes.

Obviously bitterness is a huge problem and is an extremely heavy burden in the lives of many people and of many families. Paul deals with bitterness in Ephesians chapter 4. He says in verse 31, "Get rid of all bitterness, rage and anger, brawling and slander, along with every form of malice." One day when I was a pastor in the Little Rock, Arkansas area, I was on my way to Little Rock to visit a patient at a large Catholic hospital. On my way I listened to a preacher on the radio, and he talked about this particular verse. I was very interested, because my wife and I had had an uncomfortable argument before I left for the hospital. The preacher said that (using verse 31) bitterness is when we get hurt and internalize it, rage is when that hurt becomes a seething fire inside, and anger is when we express ourselves in an angry way with another person. Brawling occurs when we get into an argument with that other person, and slander is when we leave the argument and go away and talk badly about one another. Notice that it all starts in this verse with bitterness. I believe the radio preacher is right, and that bitterness leads to a multitude of other problems and sins. If we can "nip bitterness in the bud" and cut it off, we can avoid a multitude of sins and other problems.

The Book of Job is perhaps the oldest book in the Bible. The character of Job is well known by many people, because we relate so well to his numerous problems. Chapters one and two show several ways Job was hurt and ways he could have been bitter, yet he chose not to be. Remember this in your Christian journey: everybody gets hurt, but everybody doesn't have to get bitter. Probably in the course of your life you will be bitter, just as I have been bitter. Everybody is going to get hurt regularly, but everybody does not have to be bitter regularly. We can overcome bitterness, and we can forgive.

Job's five opportunities to be bitter are all shown in chapters 1 and 2, except for the last one. Job's first experience of hurt and temptation to bitterness came when he began to lose all that he owned. Job was a wealthy man, and thieves and rustlers began to steal what he owned (Job 1:14 and following). A lot of people get bitter when they lose what they own. It's funny how our hearts are tied so closely to the possessions we have, and for someone to take them away (or for an act of God to take them away) creates doubt and sometimes bitterness. It certainly creates hurt.

The second way Job was hurt and could have become bitter occurred in Job 1:18. His sons and daughters were having a family gathering and a meal, and the wind struck the house at all four corners. It collapsed and killed all of his sons and daughters. In one mighty swoop, in an apparent act of God, Job's family members were destroyed. What an awesome scene! It reminds me of the earthquake that struck Haiti in January 2010, where 200,000 to 300,000 people were killed. Many of them were killed just like Job's children when buildings collapsed on them. Many people in Haiti are hurting physically, but you can count on it that many people are also hurting emotionally with bitterness. A lot of people are hurt when they lose somebody they love in a accident or something that appears to be an act of God.

The third way Job was hurt and could have gotten bitter was in Job 2:7 when Job was afflicted by the devil with painful sores all over his body. Job could not even scratch his nose without irritating a painful sore. I'm not sure what the sores were, but it sounds like they may have been carbuncles or risons. We simply know that they were painful sores. Job could not lie down or sit down comfortably. Of course his feelings were hurt. God could have prevented this from happening, and Job could potentially have gotten bitter. Everybody gets sick so everybody is hurt at one time or another with painful sickness. It is a good opportunity to be bitter. I just received an e-mail from a good friend today and he told me he had the H1N1 virus, or the flu. This kind of flu kills some people and that could happen to my friend. I don't mean to be morbid. Such ailments strike all of us. It will cause us to be hurt (maybe at God), and some of us will get bitter because of it.

The fourth reason Job could have been bitter was when his wife came to him in Job 2:9 and said, "Curse God and die!" Mrs. Job must have been quite a character. Job had lost most everything he owned. He lost his sons and daughters, and now he had lost his health. So his wife came to him and said, "Why don't you curse God and die, Job!" If I had been Job, I probably would have gotten my feelings hurt by this rebuke! "Job, your God is not good to you, so why don't you ask him to kill you," in other words. A lot of people are desperately hurt very deeply because of marital trouble. When I was in seminary, my wife and I had two years of very difficult marriage trouble. No one else was involved. But the sin of bitterness, anger, and a bad relationship was in the pot boiling at the Wilkes home. When we got past those two years, God worked in a great way in our home. I knew that God had saved my marriage and that we could have lost something precious. This kind of relationship certainly causes bitterness very often.

The fifth way Job could have become bitter was when he was hurt by his friends. Job 2:11 tells us that Job's three friends

Eliphaz, Bildad, and Zopher came to be a support to Job, but in later chapters they wound up being deeply critical of Job. They criticized him to his face and accused him of not really loving God. A lot of people are deeply hurt and often become bitter when their friends turn on them. I have had friends that turned on me, that criticized me, and that spoke against me to other friends. I am sure that you have, too. In fact I believe this is the most regular way I find myself being hurt and bitter at times.

I was speaking at a revival meeting in southwestern Kentucky in a town on the Mississippi River. I was driving back and forth almost every night from Memphis to the church where I was speaking. One night I decided to invite a couple of seminary students to go with me. We had a good time, and on the way home my friend Pat was driving. I was sitting in the back seat talking to him. I looked up and saw a dead dog in the middle of the road, but I was too late to warn Pat. We hit that dog hard on the bottom of my car. We were still able to drive, but we made it back into Memphis late. I went into the seminary the next day for work and my car was barely running. I took the car to be repaired at a repair shop that I had used before. A man called me about four o'clock that afternoon and told me it was my transmission that was messed up, and that they did not fix transmissions. I didn't know what to do. I got in my car and headed toward Kentucky. I got to the northern part of Memphis and the car was making all kinds of funny sounds. I prayed, and said, "God what should I do?" Right after I prayed I saw a small transmission shop. I pulled in and asked them if they could help me and they said they could. There were just 2 men that worked in this shop, men I will call Bob and Jim.

I began to talk to Bob about my problem and that I was speaking at a revival meeting. He understood, and he appeared to be a Christian. He kept leaving my car to answer the telephone, and I began to get the impression the he had a girlfriend. Bob was probably in his thirties. As I talked to him more about his life and circumstances, I found out that he was working out of his field. He had a college degree in another field. He was divorced and married again and separated from his second wife. Things were not good in Bob's life. As I talked to him about Jesus and his relationship to Him, he began to ask me what he should do in light of his circumstances. He went to answer the telephone again, and I was left with Jim who was a worker there.

Jim and I had a little chat, and I determined that he was not a Christian, but he was hungry to be a Christian. There was no one else in the building. So we stepped aside in a private place and Jim prayed to give his life to Jesus while I guided him. It was a wonderful experience. When Bob came back out I told him that Jim had given his life to Christ, and that since he was a Christian, he should be able to help Jim. Bob said, "Somebody needs to help me." I walked out back while they were fixing my transmission and began to consider how he could deal with his hurt and bitterness. Nine years earlier Bob had been deeply hurt when his brother, who was an Assembly of God minister, was in an accident and killed. Some drunks were riding in the other car. They hit Bob's brother's vehicle and killed him. Then they took their cans and bottles of liquor and threw them into Bob's brother's car to make it look like he was at fault. Bob was so hurt that he got bitter. I probably would have too! This was nine years before I met him.

I came back into the building and told Bob what he was going to have to do. He was all ears and was listening carefully to what I had to say. I told him that in order to get rid of his bitterness, first, he was going to have to admit to God and himself that he really was bitter. Second he would need to do a very difficult thing. He would have to take responsibility that it was his fault he was bitter—not God's fault, not somebody else's fault, and not circumstances' fault. It was his fault. Third, he needed to repent. He should simply ask God to forgive his sins and change him afresh, so he could serve the Lord. Fourth he needed to surrender his life to Jesus afresh and anew, and ask the Holy Spirit to take control of his life. Everybody gets hurt, and it is not wrong to be hurt. It's wrong to let it seethe and become bitterness. Remember this also: everybody gets bitter occasionally; but I am not excusing sin. I'm just stating facts—we must learn to catch ourselves. We can tell when we are getting bitter, and we must repent and go through these essential steps.

Bitterness causes all kinds of problems. It causes physical problems, emotional problem, spiritual problems, and it probably can be stated truthfully that some people die of bitterness because of all their problems.

## The Blessing of Getting Better

SOME CHRISTIANS, NO MATTER what is thrown at them, continue to have victory and thrive through all their problems. My mother and her early life have been an example for me. When she was in her early thirties, my father died in a car wreck and only 5 months later her mother passed away slowly because of cancer. I was a young boy at this time, but I can still remember my mother's attitude of being able to continue on not matter what. Nothing was going to defeat her, and she continued to go on. She and my father had become Christians as young adults just a few years before my daddy died.

In Ephesians 4:32 scripture tells us, "Be kind and compassionate to one another, forgiving each other, just as in Christ God forgave you." This verse comes immediately following a verse that deals with bitterness, anger, and hatred. There's a contrast here in this portion of God's word. Some people are bitter and angry, and other people are kind and compassionate. It's not that we're made that way, and it is not that we have a background that forces us to be angry. The truth is that we choose to be kind and compassionate. Jesus was hurt over and over, but He chose to be kind anyway.

In one of the churches that I pastored, there was a young man who had curly hair—almost an afro. He was not an African-American, but he had a big head of hair. He was one of our Sunday school teachers and he taught the adults in our small mission church. I will call him John. John was a salesman and had a family with two daughters—one was a teenager and one was twelve. John was a good Sunday school teacher. He loved the Bible and he taught it clearly. I also found out he was a man of prayer. Not long after I became John's pastor, I found out he was going through a devastating experience; his wife left him for another man. In my understanding of devastating experiences, for a young man to have his wife leave him is one of the most hurtful. Although John was deeply hurt, he continued to serve the Lord. We formed a prayer group of four young men to pray for revival, and John was always at that meeting where we prayed. As we prayed, God met with us in a way that I had never experienced in my life. We were praying for revival in our church. We were desperate for revival in our church. Six months later we saw genuine revival in our little church (that soon was not so little). Through all that experience John continued to serve Jesus.

I know there were times when John came home from work and did things like kick the refrigerator door, throw the cat across the room, and even scream at his children, but I never heard about those. I just heard and saw him continue faithfully to serve the Lord. Much later I was astounded when I discovered that John's wife had returned. I watched real Christianity at work as he openly and lovingly embraced her and welcomed her back into the home. I got to know his wife better, and she even did some typing for me when I was doing graduate work.

Before long John's wife left him again—with a different man. This time we heard they were together in upstate New York. Amazingly, John continued to serve Jesus. He kept praying, and he kept serving the Lord in front of his daughters.

John's wife came back to him a second time. He opened his arms and his heart and let her come home. I heard about them again years later. They had moved, and they were together serving God as a couple. Bitterness would have cut this miracle short. But God had His way in their lives.

During World War II, Corrie Ten Boom and members of her family were incarcerated by the Nazi authorities. Corrie and her sister Betsy suffered much at the hands of the Germans in war camps, and Betsy eventually died in a Nazi war camp. Betsy repeatedly told her sister Corrie that she should forgive and love everyone. When the war ended Corrie was released from prison, and she took up where she left off in Amsterdam. As she began to serve the Lord, she began to write and God used her in a mighty way before her death many years after the war. Corrie Ten Boom could have been extremely bitter. She "deserved" to be bitter and angry and to hate others because of what had happened to her and her sister. Corrie loved Jesus and she was able to forgive and love her enemies just as her sister Betsy had encouraged her to do.

You and I have experiences that may not be as dramatic as John's or Corrie Ten Boom's, but our experiences can nonetheless be painful. We can give way to bitterness, or we can be kind and compassionate as Jesus wants us to be and was Himself. Again bitterness can destroy us. It can put us in an early grave. It can destroy our relationships with our family and those closest to us, but it doesn't have to. God will enable us to overcome bitterness.

Remember our friend Bob at the transmission shop? Bob listened while I was telling him how to overcome his bitterness. He looked at me without closing his eyes and said, "Steve, I guess I just did." What he meant was that he had just given his life back to Jesus Christ. I watched this young man be transformed by the power of God in a matter of hours. Before I left his shop Bob's life was already coming back together. He wanted to go to church with me, even that night. I stayed in touch with him before I left Memphis for the summer, and I discovered he was back in church, his attitude was different, and the bitterness was gone. It's a supernatural act, but God can do it in your life and in mine if we let him. Don't let bitterness ruin your life. It's a spiritual problem that committed Christians share with the rest of the world.

# 5

# SPIRITUAL WARFARE

## *There is a Battle!*

MY FAMILY HAS BEEN very involved in America's wars. My Dad turned twenty about the time World War II began. He and one of my uncles and another man slipped away and joined the Navy. My father became a Navy medic, and he was attached to the Marine Corps. He was sent to the South Pacific and was present during the battle at Guadalcanal. I was only five when he died, so he didn't tell me a lot about the war. I've had to hear some of his stories secondhand from others, but he did leave scores and scores of photographs which he took in the South Pacific. I remember looking through them and seeing stacks of bodies riddled by bullets. They depicted horrible scenes and showed war in the raw. I have been told that the fighting at Guadalcanal was the most intense fighting of World War II.

My mother's brother, my Uncle Edward, was an officer in the Army in World War II where he fought with General George Patton. It was a tough war in Europe.

My former stepfather was in the Army during the Korean conflict. He was a fifty caliber machine gun sergeant. When I was a boy he used to tell me stories, gory stories from the war. He knew a man who was captured by the Chinese. They cut off his legs and made him walk in the snow of Korea to spare his life.

My first cousin fought in Vietnam. In fact he became a Christian in a foxhole in Vietnam. However he was never the same after he came home following his second tour of duty in Vietnam.

I missed being directly involved in a war because of my age and the fact that I was in college during Vietnam. However, the tenth grader, who helped me give my life to Jesus, died in the Vietnam conflict.

War is no stranger to my family. Today, I am a committed Christian trying to serve Jesus to the best of my ability through His power. I am engaged in a great war. I have experienced spiritual warfare on a personal level here at home and on foreign soil as I attempted to help start new churches overseas.

Sometime early in my ministry, I noticed that American Christians have created what I call "spiritual fads" out of some of the theological trends of the day. The first fad I observed was the "second coming fad" during the Jesus movement of the late sixties and early seventies. I have heard that Hal Lindsey's book, *The Late Great Planet Earth*, sold 28 million copies by 1990. It was all about Jesus' second coming. It was a good book, but it caught the wave of this spiritual fad and became a phenomenal best seller.

The second fad that I noticed was one centering on the devil. Again author Hal Lindsey wrote a popular book entitled *Satan Is Alive and Well on Planet Earth*. There have been several other fads since that time that I have observed—a fad on the family, one on spiritual gifts and many others. Here I want to discuss what is no longer a spiritual fad in our country—the biblical teaching and practical outworking of spiritual warfare in the life of the Christian.

## Examples of Spiritual Warfare

ONE OF THE FIRST clear examples of spiritual warfare that I personally observed occurred when I was a pastor right out of seminary. We needed a part-time staff member to lead music and work with our young people, and I had met a young man named Richard. He was already married, had a great heart for God, and was very capable. The church called Richard to serve with us while he finished college at Ole Miss. He and his wife decided to move to our town, so we began to look for a place for them to live. We were in a very small town, and there were no apartments available. We heard of a small place across the street from our church. We talked to the owner, and she was very interested in renting the place. Her daughter lived below the potential place for Richard and his family. We went to look at the apartment that had been unoccupied for years, and found that it was being used as a storage place for the family that owned it. Four of us and the owner were walking through the place when the daughter of the owner showed up. I don't remember speaking to her myself, but she spoke to Richard and his wife in a very harsh and ugly manner. She told them that she did not want them to live there. As we were strolling through the small apartment, we walked out onto an upstairs porch and saw satanic magazines on the floor. We found out later that the daughter of the owner was using the place and the magazines were hers. Tensions were high when we left, and as we talked about it, they decided that this was not the place they should live. Later, it was interesting that a house came available just across the street from where the young lady lived. All of us were certain that we were in a spiritual battle.

The most dramatic spiritual battle I have ever fought came toward the end of one of my interim pastorates. I had been preaching at this church three times a week for months when this pretty young lady walked by my podium after a service and put a note down on the podium. Later I read the note and in it she told me how much she hated me, and that she had hated me since I arrived at the church. Of course I wanted to know why she hated me, so I looked her up and this led to a discussion. She began to share with me about her life and the difficulties she had faced, including trying to kill herself, and being institutionalized. She told me that she had had an intimate affair with a pastor. I met with her, always careful to keep the door open in the pastor's study where we talked. After awhile she divulged to me that she had been a member of a witch coven during her college years. She said that she went to one of their meetings and could sense great power, so she got interested. She and a friend of hers were in that coven about a year. The friend decided to get out of the group, and the coven members killed her!

After hearing her story, it became serious business to me. I wanted to help her, and I suspected that she was demon possessed. She came to Memphis, and we met at my seminary office. I shared with her about salvation and how God could break the power of the devil which was controlling her. She revealed to me that the ring on her right hand was a different kind of wedding ring—she was married to the devil! After talking for awhile, I led her to pray to receive Jesus Christ into her life. She went along with me in the prayer, but at the time I could tell something was wrong. I could sense that her heart was not in this. I stood as I led her to pray. I held her hand, and I addressed the demons which were inside her. I could tell she wasn't very compliant. After praying to receive Christ she began to rub my hand gently with her fingers, and she scared me half to death! I knew what she had done with another pastor and I felt trapped.

She left my office, and I continued to be interim pastor of her church, but I was really afraid. I was afraid that she would try to do something to embarrass me publicly or say that I had been involved with her in an inappropriate way. On two occasions I even carried a friend so I would have a witness.

On one particular Sunday morning during the invitation I was inviting people to give their lives to Christ. This young lady was sitting on one of the front rows on the right side. There was a window in the back and the sun was coming through the window. Somehow she was able to manipulate her "satanic wedding ring," and the light streamed in my eyes and almost made me weak. I was glad that the service was almost over, because I was just stunned.

I left the church a couple of months later. My last service was on a Sunday night and after the service I received a phone call. I went to the telephone, and it was the young woman. She asked me simply, "Brother Steve, will you still help me?" I told her I would try, and I never heard from her again. I still wonder if she's possessed by demons.

It was not until I was almost forty years old that I began to take spiritual warfare seriously. One year I was going through some difficult personal battles, and a young man, whom I had helped give his life to Jesus came by the seminary to have lunch. He and I were very close friends, and I shared with him some of what I was going through. He said to me, "Steve you need to put on the armor of God." He talked with me plainly about spiritual warfare and what it could do. I began regularly, almost daily, to put on the spiritual armor found in Ephesians 6. I am fortunate that this happened before my encounter with the demon possessed young woman!

All this training and thinking about warfare became very important in my life soon. In only four years I began to make regular trips to the former Soviet Union, and I took scores of people with me. On those trips we ran into situations that could only be satanic. I was personally arrested by Russian police for preaching on the street in a town of about 75,000 people. I have discussed it in another place in this book. However it would be good to state here that this was probably a form of spiritual warfare.

A young man who was on my mission team in Poland was witnessing in a neighborhood. A neighborhood tough guy came up to my team member and said to him, "If you come back to this neighborhood, I will kill you!" What was he doing in this neighborhood? He was sharing the gospel of Jesus Christ. He was seeing a good many people give their lives to Jesus. It was probably spiritual warfare. Here is a principle that should be noted: Sometimes there is spiritual warfare and sometimes you just suspect spiritual warfare. It's a battle that often is not clear.

I have been privileged for over thirty years to know a great Christian brother who is now one of my colleagues at the seminary where I teach. He and I both teach in the missions department. While I was in graduate school, I was his assistant for about three years. I have heard him talk repeatedly about his wonderful experiences as a missionary in Malawi, East Africa. One time he was cursed by a witch doctor and havoc broke loose against him. Right after that he was walking on the boat dock that he built on Lake Malawi, and he suddenly slipped. His feet jumped out from under him, and he landed on his head and was seriously injured. About the same time he was walking near the home he had built for his wife and five children. As he walked under a tree, his pet monkey, that his family loved dearly, jumped out of the tree and almost tore my friend's ear off. Needless to say he was again injured badly.

These are only a few examples of what spiritual warfare can be like. It can be physical, it can be emotional, it can be family related, or it can enter into areas of our life that we didn't even know about. The Bible is full of references to the devil, from the early chapters of Genesis to the end of the book of Revelation. There is obviously a cosmic conflict between God and the devil, but that conflict is also against groups of Christians and certain individual Christians. For instance, Paul struggled with the devil and wrote about it in his epistles. The struggle continues today! Probable the best known passage concerning spiritual warfare is in Ephesians 6. If you check out the passage you will note in verse 12 alone that the word "against" is used five times. In other words we are fighting against Satan and his demons.

Most committed Christians have paid attention to Ephesians 6, read the passage, and perhaps even studied it. What concerns me is not that we know there is a spiritual warfare going on; my concern is that as committed Christians most of us ignore that same spiritual warfare. We know the devil is after us, we know the battle is real, we have experienced it in a personal way sometime in the past, yet on a daily basis we ignore the command in Ephesians 6:13, "Therefore put on the full armor of God." The language in this passage lets us know this is not a one-time putting on of the armor of God. When we are saved, the armor does not suddenly snap in place and stay there the rest of our lives. We are to regularly put on the armor of God so we will "Be able to stand our ground, and after you have done everything, to stand" (Ephesians 6:13).

Six pieces of armor are mentioned from verse 14 through verse 18. The passage in Ephesians tells us in verse 14 to put on the belt of truth, and to put on the breastplate of righteousness. In verse 15 we are to have our feet ready to share the gospel. Certainly evangelism creates an atmosphere for spiritual warfare. In verse 16 we are told to take up the shield of faith and the helmet of salvation. Finally we are to turn from defensive pieces of armor to the only offensive piece of armor. In verse 17 we are told to take up the sword of the Spirit, and that sword is the Word of God.

Two major schools of thought compete when it comes to spiritual warfare in American evangelical Christianity. The first group of Christians tends to find demons "behind every bush." They are looking for spiritual conflict to be behind almost every situation, especially problems. The second group of Christians believes in the biblical teaching of Satan, demons, and spiritual warfare. However they tend to believe it theologically and ignore it practically. Somewhere between these two viewpoints is the truth. Of course there are spiritually fallen angels which have been loosed like a roaring lion set free from a cage. We must remember that every problem we have as committed Christian is not due to the activity of a demon. Remember, we fight three enemies—the world, the flesh, and the devil. Sometimes it's much easier to blame a problem on the devil than it is to recognize that the problem may be our own flesh.

Frank Peretti has written several novels that deal with demons. I read his book *This Present Darkness* several years ago. In the book Peretti does an excellent job of telling his story. He also sets up a theological system which depicts demons being almost everywhere. In the book he tells the story of a small college in a small town and how that town and college where attacked by the forces of evil. It's a wonderful read, and Peretti may not have intended to set up a theological system of demonology, but as a result many people have taken the book to be a pattern which we can use today. I've heard people talk about Peretti's writings as if they were biblical theology. I like to read Frank Peretti, but some have taken him much too literally when it comes to spiritual warfare.

Ephesians 6:18, the verse following the armor of God passage, tells believers to pray on all occasions and with all kinds of prayers. A major part of spiritual warfare takes place when we pray. Victories are won when we pray, and the devil and his demons flee when we pray.

Another key passage concerning the spiritual warfare we fight as believers is found in 2 Corinthians 10:3-4. The passage in the NIV says "For though we live in the world, we do not wage war as the world does. The weapons we fight with are not the weapons of the world. On the contrary, they have divine power to demolish strongholds." This passage does not mention the devil or demons, but it does talk about war, weapons, and strongholds. The consensus of many evangelicals is that this is a clear passage on spiritual warfare. The bottom line teaching of this passage concerns demolishing strongholds. Strongholds seem to be a habit, a thought, a pattern of thinking, a traumatic experience from the past... It concerns something in the mind and spirit of the believer which needs to be destroyed.

Early in my marriage I noticed that my wife had a tendency to try to control me in a subtle way. She is a sweet Christian believer, and much of this occurred before she had given her life to Jesus at age 26. From her past I discovered that the ladies in her family have a tendency to try to control their husbands. I could tell after years of thinking, praying, and studying about this that there was something that just was not right. In the fall of our eleventh year of marriage, I got very concerned about this matter of control. I did not want to control her, and I knew she didn't try to do this to me, but it still existed in our marriage. That fall, for two or three months, we went through intense discussions and prayer about this matter. One night in our home in Arkansas I knelt beside Carol's chair with her permission and prayed that God would destroy this stronghold of control. This was no theory. This involved my marriage. During the course of that fall something wonderful happened, and our marriage has never been the same. I even developed a talk for my seminary students and titled it: "The Controlling Woman Syndrome". This is a clear example of spiritual warfare in the home.

The issues of Ephesians 6 and the armor of God bring up several questions which are not clear but can be answered with biblical and common sense. First, how do we put on the armor of God? Undoubtedly it is to be put on through the prayer life of the individual Christian. Second, how often should we put on the armor of God? The Bible doesn't give us an answer. The answer is simply, often. I try to make it a practice to put on the armor of God daily during my quiet time and when I surrender to the filling of the Holy Spirit. Third, does a Christian not already have the armor of God on since he belongs to Christ? That is a good question, except Paul was addressing believers when he told them to put on the armor of God. Obviously Christians need to suit up regularly for spiritual battle. For those who may be skeptical about the activity of demons or Satan in our lives today I would remind you that the Lord Jesus Christ used much of His ministry time dealing with the devil, and demons. Over and over Jesus cast demons from people, healed sickness caused by demons, and recognized that the problem people were having was satanic.

Mark 5 tells the story of the Gadarene demoniac. More than likely no one else will ever encounter something as dramatic as what happened here, but it is in the written Word of God. Jesus encountered a man who was a demoniac; he was naked, he was living in a graveyard, he was cutting himself with stones, frightening people, and crying out in what must have been a deafening wail. Jesus recognized this man was not crazy, but he was controlled by demons. In only a few words, the Lord delivered the man and sent the demons into some pigs. It is unbelievable, but the very people who had been frightened by this demoniac begged Jesus to go away from their area. He did and left without ministering in their region.

This story was not a figment of someone's imagination. It was not Jesus accommodating himself to the thinking of the times in which he lived (as some have suggested). It was not Jesus being ignorant of reality. The story shows Jesus delivering a poor man from the demons which controlled him.

The question we must ask is simply, does this kind of thing happen today? I would ask another question to help us answer the first. What has changed? God hasn't changed, the nature of men hasn't changed, the devil hasn't changed, and demons haven't changed. Mark 5 and the Gadarene demoniac story could happen somewhere in the world today. God has given us power over the enemy if we will only use His power.

Elisha was a quiet, powerful prophet of God in the Old Testament. His story is found in 2 Kings 6. Elisha had a servant named Gehazi. Gehazi saw the huge forces of the King of Aram and was terribly alarmed. Elisha told him not to be afraid. In 2 Kings 6:16 he stated, "Those who are with us are more than those who are with them." This is the Old Testament counterpart of the wonderful verse in 1 John 4:4 which says, "Because the One who is in you is greater than the one who is in the world." This is a clear reference to our enemy the devil. Elisha knew that the angels of God were much more powerful than the forces of King Aram. Elisha prayed in 2 Kings 6:17, "O Lord, open his eyes so that he may see." Then God did open Gehazi's eyes, and he saw that the hills were full of the horses and chariots of God.

You and I need to see that there really is spiritual warfare in our world. There are demons who would like to hurt us; however God is stronger. First John 4:4 has for decades been comforting to me, "Because the One who *is* in you is greater than the one who is in the world."

What happens when we ignore spiritual warfare? It is a serious problem. First, we go to war and don't even know where the battle is. The battle belongs to the Lord, and His battle is with our enemy, the devil. We should be strong, alert, and biblically smart. Second, we will encounter resistance in our

Christian lives and ministry and will often have no idea the cause of it. As a result of this ignorance, we will not be able to deal with the enemy and the problems we are facing.

What difference does it make if we do not practice spiritual warfare and are not aware of it? First, we are disobedient to the Word of God if we do not put on the armor of God and resist the devil as we are told in James 4:7, "Resist the devil and he will flee from you." Before we can resist we must note verse six, which says, "Submit yourselves to God." Submitted Christians, full of the power of the Holy Spirit, are able to resist the devil and be involved in spiritual warfare.

Second, the protection which comes from the spiritual armor of God is not ours. It is His, and it is powerful. Imagine going into a battle without a gun, helmet, and other protective gear. It just should not happen. Neither should believers go to battle without the armor of God.

Third, when we do put on the armor of God we have protection from our enemy, and we can see victory. God has planned for us to experience victory.

Many Christians ignore spiritual warfare. They may plan "someday" to learn about the enemy. Some go to the other extreme and begin thinking there are demons behind every problem they have. As you live your Christian life, you will make the discovery that sometimes you are your greatest enemy! Balance is very important, especially in dealing with spiritual warfare.

Just after His baptism Jesus went into the wilderness and fasted for forty days where He dealt with the temptations of Satan. Scripture teaches that He went into the wilderness in the fullness of the Spirit, and He came out of the wilderness in the power of the Holy Spirit. Temptation may not be pleasant, but it yields powerful spiritual fruit. We are strengthened by the Holy Spirit when we are tempted by the devil. Don't ignore your enemy!

# 6

# LUST

## *Controlling Desires*

WHEN I WAS A PASTOR, rumors began to fly about a fellow pastor. The rumor was that this pastor and a certain lady were involved in an affair. I had church members who lived very close to the accused woman, so I felt an obligation to involve myself and maybe help. I asked a committed Christian man that lived nearby if he thought there was anything to the rumors about his neighbor and this pastor. He said, "No," and he was emphatic about it. However, he did tell me that he had been in a social situation when the pastor and this woman were present, and there was laughter and raucous talk about certain body parts unique to females. He told me that the pastor was not doing the talking, but he was there when it happened. He did not say anything, but sleazy talk continued while he was present.

This raised my suspicions about the truth of the rumors, but I did not act for a while. Later, while having my quiet time. I was lying on the carpet in our den, reading in the book of Galatians. I came to Galatians 6:1 where the Bible says, "Brothers, if someone is caught in a sin, you who are spiritual should restore him gently. But watch yourself, or you also may be tempted," God began to work in my heart, and I felt strongly compelled to call my preacher friend. He had moved to another state, but I was able to find his phone number and I called him. I told him who I was, and I told him what the situation was—that rumors were flying about him and marital infidelity. He strongly denied any wrong doing. Of course I did not accuse him—I just told him about the situation and that I wanted to help. He talked on, and on, and on for about 45 minutes. We discussed what to do, how bad the rumors were, and so on. I tried to help. He was a good brother, and I had known him for a number of years.

A couple of months later, I ran into him at a convention, which was meeting in Pittsburgh. We got on an elevator together, and it was very uncomfortable. That did not let me know for sure that he was guilty, but my suspicions were up.

Later I heard that he had repeated his immorality in a new church, and I knew that the rumors from before were probably true. My heart was broken, but I did not know what else to do.

Not long ago I heard what is probably an old story. This old Christian man was having a conversation with a young Christian man. The younger man was obviously concerned and asked the older man, "How old do you have to get before lust is no longer a problem." The older man smiled and said, "You're going to have to ask someone older than I am to get an answer to that!" This humorous story illustrates the truth of a very important Christian matter; sexual lust is not just a problem for younger people, it remains a problem all our lives and committed Christians need to learn to deal with it.

Today soft porn (are we sure it's soft?) appears on television and even in our daily newspapers. I have seen an ad lately, for several days in a row, in our hometown paper which showed a young lady in an extremely scanty bikini. Movies are still rated R, PG, etc . . ., but I wonder if the categories are more lenient than they used to be. The Internet has brought the availability of hard core porn to the great majority of American households. We can bemoan these things and complain about them until the cows come home, yet we might as well admit it—they affect Christians, too!

The basic problem seems to be that committed Christians do not want to admit that we have a lust problem, either from self-deceit or pride. We Christians, who are trying to live for Jesus, just cannot imagine ourselves wrapped up in lust. I even heard of one Christian worker who told another fulltime Christian worker that he never had a problem with lust. That fits in the self-deceit category.

The month I graduated from seminary in 1977, I went to a huge pastor's seminar attended by about 1,000 ministers in Memphis. It was a regional pastor's seminar, so all the men were not from the Memphis area. Some of them had driven in. I think I will always remember the speaker talking about lust and saying to us pastors, "Men this will be your greatest battle." I think I already knew that he was right. However, I have discovered that many of my fellow sold-out Christians (including pastors) are extremely hesitant to talk about their own lust problem. I guess they are trying to keep up the appearance that everybody talks about— preachers are not really human. The truth is, we all know differently.

Junior Hill is my favorite evangelist, and he comes from north Alabama (my neck of the woods). While he was preaching at our seminary, his concluding message in a series of messages during our "Campus Revival" was entitled "The Shame of Neighing Horses." He took his text from Isaiah and talked about how many preachers were like the neighing horses in this passage, which were lusting after the female horses. Since my daughter owns horses and gives riding lessons, I have had the privilege of being around horses. I understand this passage better than I would have otherwise. Horses neigh when they are passionate. They are trying to communicate, and they are passionate when they lust. Junior was comparing many pastors to these neighing horses. He told two or three raw-boned stories about preachers he had known personally and their involvement in lust. A pastor told him that a well known denominational leader had sat on the platform with him at the beginning of a service, leaned over to him, and said, "Pastor which of the ladies out there in the congregation will be available to fulfill my needs this week."

I do not want to bring ridicule on those in the ministry. We all know that we are human and that some have committed sexual immorality. Many of these people are truly godly men; they have given way in a pattern of lustful thinking, and they have given in to lust. It could happen to anyone, and it certainly could happen to me. However this is a problem of committed Christians that we haven't dealt with adequately.

One of the greatest Christian leaders of the 19th century, George Mueller, said that traveling is spiritually dangerous. He said this in the context of temptation. Now that I have traveled to several different places in the world, I have begun to know what Mueller was talking about. There is much temptation when we do not know the people around us, and we are away from home.

I was in Ecuador about 2002 and had just had the joy of leading a woman to Christ in her little store. She had turned the television off and pulled the front door down most of the way. She sat down on a large bag of beans and gave me her full attention. She told us that her sister had become an evangelical Christian, and so she was open to the Lord. I shared the gospel with her and she joyfully gave her life to Jesus in prayer. I walked out of her little store and back toward our vehicles which were parked up a hill. On the way, my translator and I walked through an open air market. I handed a tract to a large African woman who was selling her goods in the market. She looked at the tract and then looked back at me and said (Gasp!), "I want you." She meant me. I laughed, and it was a relaxed laughter since I had other people with me. I said to her "Well, I am already married." She replied, "Well what does that matter?" I laughed again and said, "I am a Christian." She said "That doesn't matter. What do we do now?" By this time she had become so insistent that I was getting a little uncomfortable. I walked up the hill to our vehicle. When I got there I pulled out a piece of paper and pen and wrote down everything I could remember about the incident so I could tell my wife exactly what happened. As Mueller said, "Travel is dangerous."

Watch yourself, especially when you go out of town and particularly if you are by yourself. Motels often are seed beds of immorality. We have to be careful if we are going to live for Jesus everywhere we go. Lust is a powerful and controlling part of life. If we let ourselves go, it can destroy our testimonies, our marriages, and even our lives. Is it not interesting that venereal disease is still around and we have not whipped it yet? We still reap what we sow!

## Lust Is Personal

IN THE EARLY eighties, when I was in my thirties, I heard about so many ministers falling to lust and immorality that it really began to scare me. I did not know what to do. I knew that I was not going to let myself fall into immorality, but I guessed that those other men of God had felt the same way. So I decided to take a drastic measure. I asked God to kill me and give me a good clean heart-attack if He could see that I was going to commit immorality. I knew that I would rather die than give in, so I asked God to take me out—and I really meant it. I also asked him not to let me back out, and I have prayed that over and over. However as I got older I began to notice that heart disease is rather common in my family. It occurred to me that one day I may have a heart attack and those who had heard that I had asked God to kill me might think that I had gotten into immorality! So I changed prayers and simply asked God to kill me if I got close to immorality. I did not want to bring shame on Jesus this way.

This is such a serious matter—this thing of lust. It has been serious in my life, and I am sure it has been your life. Before I knew Christ, lust was an overwhelming thing in my life. I had no idea how to control it, nor did I try very hard. At sixteen I gave my life to Jesus, and things really changed in this area of my life. God began to give me self control, even as an older teenager.

I went to college in 1969 in the middle of the sexual revolution. Morality was changing in our land. I got away from the Lord that first year of college and again lust attacked me like a warrior. Today I am in my late fifties. I have not been unfaithful, but like Jimmy Carter admitted in 1976, I have lusted! I am not proud of it. I do not dismiss it as something everybody does (even though they do). Still, I am responsible for my actions and my thoughts.

I had two medical doctors in one of my Spiritual Formation classes several years ago. I was discussing this matter of lust, and I mentioned how it was not as big a problem after I was 43 or 44. One of the doctors said, "That's when your hormones change and decline." I did not know that, but I knew that lust was not as big a problem, and I was delighted. I really would rather die than bring shame to the name of Jesus, to my family, and to all my friends by committing immorality. This is not to say that you do not deserve to be alive if you have committed adultery or immorality. It is simply to underline the fact that it is serious—something we must flee.

## What Does God Say?

SINCE THE LATE 1980s, some in Hollywood have chosen to picture our Lord Jesus in lustful, even immoral situations. When the movie the *Last Temptation of Christ* came out in Memphis, a friend of mine, who happens to be a medical doctor, took it upon himself to personally protest the movie by himself. Once I went out and stood with him while he held his placard up and discouraged people from seeing a movie that brings great disregard to Jesus Christ.

More recently Dan Brown's book *The Da Vinci Code* and the movie which came from the book depicted Jesus in a lustful relationship with Mary Magdalene. The Bible calls this kind of speculation "blaspheme." Sadly people in western society have chosen to act like they are smarter than God.

This is the same Lord Jesus Christ who said in Matthew 5, you "You have heard that it was said, do not commit adultery. But I tell you that anyone who looks at a woman lustfully has already committed adultery with her in his heart" (Matthew 5:27-28). Since Jesus was and is God, you do not have to worry about Him committing adultery, nor do we have to be concerned that He lusted after women. Certainly, He did not.

He did tell us that if we look lustfully at a woman, we have already committed adultery in our hearts. It is pretty plain to see what this means, but sometimes it is hard to know when we have lusted. It is not lust to look at someone, and it is not lust to notice someone because they are attractive. Some have said that the first look is ok, but the second look is lust. I am not sure about that.

When we look at someone and begin to think about the possibility of having a sexual relationship with that person, we have committed adultery in our hearts. Some have said if we have committed adultery in our hearts when we lust, then we should just go ahead and commit adultery since it is no different. That is just not true.

The Ten Commandments are a standard that God has held up for over three thousand years. Included in them is the seventh commandment which tells us not to commit adultery. It does not say not to lust, even though Jesus more fully defined sexual sin to include looking with lust in our hearts. Are there degrees of sin? Some have said that all sin is equal and all are just as grievous to God. There is no doubt that God is grieved by all sin, but it seems clear, according to Scripture, that some sins are larger than others. Jesus said in John 19:11 "Therefore the one who handed me over to you is guilty of a *greater sin*." Lust is a grievous sin to God, but it's not as great a sin as committing the act of adultery. Even the act of adultery is forgivable and can be covered by grace.

A few years ago I noticed that when Paul lists several sins together he usually starts with 2 to 4 sexual sins. For instance, in Galatians 5:19 where Paul lists fourteen or fifteen sins, he begins, "Sexual immorality, impurity and debauchery. . ." In Colossians 3:5 he gives another string of sins and begins, "Put to death, therefore, whatever belongs to your earthly nature: sexual immorality, impurity, lust, evil desires and greed which is idolatry." Here is a sin list from Paul and four of them are related to lust. Obviously lust is a major problem in the eyes of God and to the writers of the Bible. We must treat it as a major problem also.

In 1 Corinthians 6:18-20, Paul plainly calls sexual immorality a sin. I have known people to say that if you love someone it's not sin to have sex with them. In this passage he says, "Flee from sexual immorality. All other sins a man commits are outside his body, but he who sins sexually sins against his own body." Our bodies, Paul says, are the temple of the Holy Spirit. If we as Christians, commit sexual sin, we have actually sinned against our own body, and God never calls any other sin a sin against our body. It is a serious matter. In Exodus 20 and Deuteronomy 5, God gave us the Ten Commandments. Both of these passages contain the command, "You shall not commit adultery. I am aware that lust is not the same as the act of adultery; however, lust, if left unchecked, leads to adultery. (James 1:15) In the New Testament Jesus tells us that lust is like the sin of adultery. In other passages God makes it clear that He is grieved by lust.

Often when we talk about lust we are talking about men lusting. Jesus did address His statement on lust to men. Perhaps

He was talking to a group of men. Is it also possible that women might be involved in the sin of lust? This discussion is in no way intended to imply that lust is the big bad sin that God does not want to forgive. If that is true, then we are in trouble. We are simply examining the fact that lust is a problem, and God talks about it in His Word. It can be tamed, so it is not a roaring lion. We are also not trying to imply that God does not use people who have lusted in the past. Of course He does or we would all be put out to pasture like an old horse. God uses sinners; God loves us even when we sin. David and Solomon both lusted in a dramatic way. David had several wives, and committed his most infamous sin when he lusted after Bathsheba and committed adultery with her. Yet God himself said of David, "He is a man after my own heart." No one else in the entire Bible is acclaimed spiritually like David. Solomon, the son of David, had hundreds of wives. Solomon was said to be the wisest man ever. He and David both fell headlong, however, into lust.

## Conclusion

YEARS AGO I READ an article that shocked me. The article was in Leadership magazine, and it dealt in a very frank way with this problem of lust. The name of the article was "The War Within: An Anatomy Of Lust" I was so taken by the article that I have copied it and used it in seminary classes. The article was unsigned and anonymous. In it the writer chronicled his horrible bout with lust. He told about traveling extensively and how he was tempted and gave in to lust. He spoke of several occasions when he sinned sexually. One of the shocking things about the article was that the author was in full time Christian work.

How can we deal with this raging bull that desires to control us and make us fall while we are trying to serve Christ? First, we must admit that it is a problem for us. At some point lust is a problem for almost everyone. We must come clean before God and admit that we have sinned—every time we give in to lust. I know that some men might say, "I would be confessing my sin all day long." Well, my advice to them is to confess it all day long if they truly long to have victory. If Jesus said for us not to do it, then it certainly is a sin if we lust. When any sin dominates our lives as Christians, we need to establish accountability with somebody who knows, understands, and loves us. When we give in to this or any other sinful problem, we should be honest and admit it to those to whom we are accountable. I can imagine somebody asking if a man should confess lust to his wife every time he lusts. After all he has committed adultery in his heart. My answer to that is simply, no! We confess our sin to Jesus. I knew some seminary students who had established an accountability practice with one another and it even included confessing each act of lust. I am afraid that's going too far. Simply confess it to the Lord.

To gain the upper hand over Satan and our lust, we need to learn a wonderful biblical truth—we have been crucified with Christ, and we are no longer to be ruled by sin. Romans 6 gives us some basic teaching on how the cross of Jesus Christ (on which we also died) gives us victory over the rule of sin in our lives. In verse 6, Paul says we are to know that we died with Christ. In verse 11 we are told to reckon, or to acknowledge, or even to state that we died with Jesus when he died on the cross. And then verse 12 says that we are to yield ourselves to the Lord. All of this is done so we as serious Christians can reign over sin instead of allowing sin to reign over us. I certainly didn't say we could get to the point where we never sin. I am simply stating what the Bible teaches, that we do not have to let sin reign over us. We still will stumble in areas like lust.

Here are some other practical suggestions. Some of them are in Scripture, and some of them are just common sense. The Bible talks about not looking on a maiden. (Job 31:1) Make it a practice when you're tempted to lust to look away from that person. Also do not go places where you know you will be tempted. I remember some of my favorite seminary students in the late 1980s talking about how they just could not go to a water park where everyone was dressed in their swimming suit. Why go places where you know you will be tempted?

Do not watch television shows that you know will tempt you. Do not look at the Internet if you cannot control where you look. These are simple ideas, but they can help a lot.

One of my favorite students that I have taught in these 26 years I will call Joe. Joe had charisma. He could write, he could speak, and he had a wonderfully supportive wife. Lust began to dominate his life. He discovered the strip joints in Memphis and went to them. Then quite suddenly he left his wife and kids for a former girlfriend. My heart was broken, and of course his wife's heart was broken. I must add that God's heart was broken too. Here was a man with promise, with an exciting future in serving the Lord and yet he abandoned it all because of lust. All of this did not make me shun him and refuse to be his friend. I loved him. My heart aches over His loss to the kingdom.

Please do not follow his example. Do not allow lust or some other sin to dominate you to the point that you abandon God and His purpose for your life.

# 7

# FEAR

## *It Must Be Conquered*

IN 1994 I LED a group of 27 people to St. Petersburg, Russia. Our purpose in going was to do evangelism to help the Russian churches. We spilt our team of 27 into 4 teams and scattered out across northwestern Russia. I was in charge of a team of 4, plus myself. We went to Sosnovy Bor, a city about 75 miles west of St. Petersburg.

The first evening we were in Sosnovy Bor, we met with the church, and I preached. I was so excited about being there that I poured my enthusiasm out in heavy doses. We started witnessing the next day, and people began to come to Christ. Russia was very open to Jesus at this time. The town had about 75,000 people and only one church, and that was the Baptist church we were working with. I led people to Christ in 2 different post offices—6 or 7 people. And I was able to lead people to Jesus on the street, at bus stops, and in several other places.

One evening the church asked our team of five to meet with "the church's young people." Young people in that area were older teenagers and young adults up to about 30. We met in an apartment. There were about 25 or 30 people in the room. It occurred to me that some of these people might not be Christians even though they were connected to the church, so I shared my testimony and preached. Two people indicated that they prayed to receive Christ. Excitement was in the air. I told the people, "Let's take this town for Christ. You are the ones with energy in this church, and you are the key." A young man right in front of me stood up, stuck his fist in the air and said, "Let's go do it now!" I said, "Let's go." About ten Russian believers and our team of five with one translator headed out to witness at about ten o'clock at night. It was not quite dark since we were there in late May, and it is 60 degrees above the equator. The darkest of night really never arrived in Sosnovy Bor in May.

I saw 4 men on the street, and I began to witness to them. Suddenly a police "paddy wagon" pulled up. A policeman came straight to me and said (in Russian), "You come with us." Of course, I complied. On the way to the paddy wagon, as we were getting in, my heart began to race and fear gripped me. I was almost controlled by the fear that overcame me. Thankfully, the police allowed the church's pastor and our translator to come with me. We went to the police station; I was already in jail, because there was no handle on the inside of the paddy wagon!

We arrived at the police station, and they wanted to see my papers. I did not have my passport with me at the time. I had left it with the missionary in St. Petersburg. Things began to get serious. They got on the phone and began to make calls—I suspected to St. Petersburg. I was asked to go down a hallway, and we went into an office. There a uniformed man (who was called the "Political Mayor") began to fill out a form. He took about an hour to do this. The truth is that I would have had a hard time even giving him answers had God not already begun to deal with my heart.

While I was waiting on the policemen to make calls, it occurred to me that I was scared to death and that just was not right. I was here to represent Jesus, we were winning people to Christ, God was working, and the leader of the group was scared. I began to pray, and I dealt with my fear the way God has taught me to deal with fear. Before long my fear subsided and within fifteen to twenty minutes of arriving at the police station, God had given me victory. I had my wits again. I was released after about two hours. When I was about to step outside, a young Russian lady from the church came out from behind some bushes and came up to me. She looked at me with big tears in her eyes and said, "Steve, I love you!" I guessed that she had seen me handing tracts out to policemen going in and out of the police station, and she was moved that I was doing (in tough circumstances) what I had told the believers they should do. God powerfully used this situation to work in the life of the Sosnovy Bor Baptist church.

People in the church had been resistant to me because of my enthusiasm. They opened their hearts and the Spirit of God swept through the church. Fear could have kept me from ministering in this situation, but God delivered me. He will do the same with any believer, including you. Fear is not to control us as believers. There is a way out of it.

There are all types of fear—not all fears are evil or bad. The fear of snakes is a healthy fear unless it becomes an obsession. I have a missionary friend who lived in Malawi for a year or so. It is my understanding that the only snakes in that part of Africa are deadly, poisonous snakes: black mambas, green mambas, cobras, etc. To be afraid of this kind of snake is smart. But the fear that I am talking about is the fear that is not the smart kind of fear. It's the fear that Jesus warned us against repeatedly when he said, "Fear not," "Fear not little flock," and "Do not be afraid." This is one of the most often repeated commands of our Lord Jesus Christ that is recorded in the gospels. Fear is not God's way for the Christian.

Further, certain types of fear are not good. In Joshua 1:6-9 the Lord gave Joshua instructions as he was about to enter the Promised Land as the new leader of the children of Israel. The Lord told him not to be afraid. In fact, close study of verses 6 to

9, reveals that God commands Joshua not to be afraid four times in four short verses. Joshua faced two major enemies; and they were not Canaanites or Philistines. His major enemies were fear and discouragement (1:9). Things have changed across the years, but people have not changed much. The major enemies we face as committed Christians today are the same enemies that Joshua faced.

Some people are afraid of riding in airplanes. My wife is a part of this crowd. She has flown several times, but she doesn't like it. She would choose to drive most places to avoid having to fly. Yet she goes to the airport with me and helps put me on airplanes. I have flown to many different places around the world. She has a genuine fear of flying, yet she faces it and does what is right.

One of the most debilitating fears we can have is the fear of other people. Everyone meets somebody that they feel uncomfortable with or even afraid of at times. However I have known a few people that seem to fear nobody. I am a seminary professor, as I said earlier, and I worked with 2 men for many years that fit this last category—they just seem to be intimated by or afraid of nobody. They are not controlled by the fear of people.

When some of the Jewish leaders in Luke 13 came to Jesus and warned him that Herod wanted to kill him, the Lord exclaimed, "Go tell that fox I will drive out demons and heal people today and tomorrow and on the third day I will reach my goal," Luke 13:32. In the next verse Jesus reveals part of His secret. He knew that he was about to die, and his death would take place in Jerusalem. Why be afraid of a person if you know you are about to die—and rise from the dead? That's an example for all of us. We too will die and rise again from the dead. There is no reason to be afraid of people, even the "Herods" in our life.

When God began to teach me some lessons on fear, I was in my early thirties, and I was a pastor. One of the means that God used was the game of softball. We had a softball team in our church, and our team was the only church team in an industrial league. Of course the industrial teams didn't want a bunch of church guys to beat them. However, we did beat most of them. I found myself playing second base. Most of my life I have played outfield when I played baseball or softball, but this time was different. The reason I played outfield in years past had been mainly because I was afraid of grounders. Grounders can hurt you! They can bounce up in an instant and bloody your nose or blacken your eye. They can really hurt you! God was teaching me about fear, however, and I applied it to softball. Now if you have ever played softball, you know that softballs are not soft, they are very hard. They are about as hard as a baseball, just bigger. I made up my mind that I had rather be hit in the face or anywhere else by a softball than be afraid of it. When the larger and better batters came to the plate on the opposing team I learned to go in on them or get closer to them and to yell loudly "Hit it to me, hit to me." An onlooker might say, "You are going to get hit. You are going to get hurt and you should back up." If they asked me about this I would simply tell them that I would rather be hurt than be afraid of the softball. We played several games that year where I caught some hot grounders, and I missed some, but I never really got hurt. It is amazing that most of the things we fear never happen.

The same is true in the spiritual realm. You may develop a fear of demons, but most of what you imagine is never going to happen. I want to be transparent and honest with you about fear. I have fear grip me occasionally and almost paralyze me—just like it did when I was under arrest in Russia. When I am flying in jets at 30,000 feet and turbulence begins to shake the plane all over, I really get afraid. Only a couple of years ago I was flying with some of my colleagues at the seminary and we experienced some rather dramatic turbulence. At least I thought it was dramatic, and I was gripped by fear. I looked around and my friends were acting like nothing had happened.

Fear is real, and fear can be lack of faith. When we are trusting God we don't have to be afraid. No wonder the Lord Jesus spoke so often about it. I've learned that when fear controls my life that I have stepped out of the perfect will of God. In other words God doesn't want me to do this. He doesn't want me to give in to fear. It does happen to me, to you and to everyone who is a committed Christian. When it does happen and fear controls us and begins to dominate our life, we have stepped into an area of disobedience. The Lord said not to do that.

If one character in the Bible never had to deal with fear, it would appear to be Paul the Apostle. You can read much about Paul in Scripture, because he wrote so many of the books of the New Testament. In the book of Acts, it seems like Paul never experienced fear. He was bold when he was arrested. He kept trusting God. If you look in Acts chapter 18, however, you will find a little story about Paul at Corinth. The ministry was going well, and Paul was preaching wherever he had the opportunity. I love the passage that says Paul went to the market and preached to whoever happened to be there. I have done that several places in the third world. Paul was doing this kind of preaching, witnessing, and working with the Christians when God began to work in a powerful way.

Crispus, the leader of the Jewish synagogue received Christ. Acts 16:8 says that when Crispus give his life to Jesus, his entire household did also. Often households included many people. This would not be hundreds, but it could be a score of people or more. So Crispus and a good group of people who were Jews gave their lives to Jesus Christ. You can imagine that the rest of the synagogue was terribly upset. Crispus was their leader! The leader of the synagogue had become a Christian, so there must have been quite an uproar in Corinth. Just after this we are told that Paul had a vision one night. The Lord came to him and spoke to him, "Do not be afraid; keep on speaking, do not be silent. For I am with you, and no one is going to attack and harm you, because I have many people in this city" (Acts 18:9-10.)

When God was teaching me about fear He led me to these verses and to this story. I began to study the passage, and saw that it seemed to be a pattern for dealing with fear. First of all, the Lord told Paul to stop being afraid. It can be assumed from this text that Paul had experienced fear—he had been afraid. So Jesus came to him and said, "Paul stop doing what you are doing—drop the fear." In other words, Paul was led by the Lord Himself to see that his fear was wrong. I began to see that God wants us to confess as sin the fear that controls our lives. I'm sure that is what He wants us to do, because the Lord said not to do it. I grew up in Alabama, and where I grew up I was taught that if God said don't do something and I do it, it is sin. When we are controlled by fear, we have slipped away from the control of the Lord, and we need to repent.

The Lord continued speaking to Paul and said to him in the last part of verse 9, "keep on speaking, do not be silent." After a while I could see this clearly: when we are controlled by fear, we stop doing what is right. The fear keeps us from doing it and here Jesus tells Paul, "Don't be afraid. Keep doing what you are afraid of." In other words head toward your fear in order to see the fear fall.

One year in the spring when I was learning these lessons, I was jogging on the edge of a golf course near my home. It was around April. Trees were budding, birds were singing, and flowers were coming out. As I was jogging it occurred to me, "It's the snake time of year." I became suddenly aware that it was beautiful, but it was also time for cottonmouths, rattlesnakes, etc. to be crawling, and I was running on the edge of the woods. God was teaching me how to deal with my fear, so I said to myself, "This fear is not going to control me this year." I turned toward the woods on the edge of the golf course and began to run into the woods jumping over logs, disregarding any creatures that might have been there, and I found myself shouting, "Bite me!" Now, I know that snakes can't understand English, but they certainly can hear us, and I demanded in my "Jesus voice" that they go ahead and bite me. I would rather be snake bitten than to be controlled by fear—literally! I don't want to live my life under the influence of Satan or the flesh or any circumstances that cause me to live in fear. Of course I will succumb to fear, but I do not want it to control my life. I will not allow that to happen. That is not what the control of Jesus leads us to. Thank God we do not have to be controlled by fear. Back in Acts 18:10 Jesus said to Paul, "I am with you and no one is going to harm you." I have learned to confess (even if it is under my breath) the fact that Jesus is with me. I may not feel His presence, I may not see the evidences of God working in my life, but He promised that He would be. When Jesus gave the Great Commission, He told us to go into all the world and make disciples, and then He said, "I am with you always." We can count on the fact that Jesus goes with us.

One more idea thrills me in this great passage of Scripture. In verse 10 Jesus concludes by saying, "I have many people in this city." Peace comes instead of fear when I realize that the things which may make me afraid—spiritual warfare, strong personalities, etc.—will not overcome the power of Christ working in and through me. Jesus also promised results. We will see harvest at some point if we keep on. Fear can keep us from seeing the harvest, but we do not have to give in to fear.

These key ideas have helped me overcome fear. I have shared them with mission teams I have led around the world. Before we begin to witness, usually I will bring a devotional to my team using this passage and show them that they don't have to be afraid. If they are afraid, they can repent, and God will break the power of fear and the hold it has over them. I have seen it work in several lives.

I shared these ideas on fear with a group of missionaries and missionary reps who had come to our church for a mission conference. Before the evening services we had devotional times for the missionaries, and one day I spoke on fear and emphasized the fear of witnessing. I told the missionary group that in our busyness to promote missions we can ignore sharing Christ ourselves. I shared with them that it was sin if it was because of fear that we cease to witness. Later in the conference one of the most outgoing men in the group came to me and with a humble spirit confessed that God had moved on him while I was speaking about the fear of witnessing. Even though he was bold in the Philippines where he served, he had become afraid of witnessing back in the states. When he repented, God freed him from that fear. God will do the same for you and me if we follow His simple instructions. Fear is such a culprit and a mean taskmaster, and it causes committed Christians to lose their joy. Galatians 4:15 says, "What has happened to all your joy?" When we are controlled by fear, we are not controlled by the joy of the Holy Spirit, and the mark of a Christian should be joy. Fear keeps us from serving God in big ways because we are afraid of failure. Fear even keeps us from pursuing God's will when we know what he wants.

So it's clear that fear is not only a problem—it's a sinful problem. It's a controlling problem. It's a problem that everybody faces, but it's a problem that every committed Christian can overcome by using biblical principles and submitting to the power of the Holy Spirit. When fear controls you in your witnessing life, in other areas of service, or even in simple, natural activities like walking in the woods, you don't have to give in to fear. When you realize it is controlling you, stop. Draw away even if it is in your mind and confess that fear as sin. Remember Jesus said often, "Do not be afraid." Then ponder what it is you are afraid of and make plans to do the very thing you fear. If you are afraid of witnessing, go to a restaurant, go in the restroom, take a tract out, put it on the counter, and run! It's a start. It's a beginning to help you get over your fear. Remember, fear is not faith. If you are going to walk with Jesus, you've got to walk by faith.

# 8

# WHO ARE WE IN CHRIST?

## *Discovering Our Identity*

SEVERAL YEARS AGO I was speaking at a church a couple of hours away from my home. Just before I got up to speak, a middle age man who was a member of the church sang a song which essentially said, "I'm just a sinner saved by grace." The song went on and on about how terrible we are and how great God is to take us into His family. I don't doubt the truth that God is wonderful and that outside of Christ we are horrible, condemned, and low down sinners. But in Christ is this really who we are?

After the song I brought a message which taught truths similar to those contained in this chapter. The man who sang came up to me and said, "Well, I guess you don't like the song I sang." I assured him that I did like the song and that what I was trying to say in my sermon was that God does like us, love us, and accept us when we're in Christ—when we are saved.

Around 1980 I was at a large Bible conference in Fort Worth, Texas and had the privilege to hear Pastor Peter Lord from Florida share a message he called "Turkeys and Eagles." I was stunned by the content of this message. What Peter Lord had shared was essentially that God accepts us the way we are and that we are, not just a bunch of sinners after we become Christians. At the time I was going to grad school, and when I got back to the seminary for my studies, I found out the fame of the message given by Peter Lord had preceded me—and that it was quite controversial. Some of the things which Peter Lord said had been taken wrongly. Some thought that he was saying that Christians no longer had to sin at all. That is not at all what he intended his message to portray. He was saying that Christians are not "Just sinners saved by grace."

It really wasn't until about five years later that God spoke resoundingly to my heart from the Bible concerning this idea of being accepted in Christ. In 1980 there was a small movement among evangelical Christians in which people were embracing the idea of God's love and acceptance of the believer just as he is. I never heard anyone say that Christians don't sin any more. Those who have studied the teachings and doctrines of evangelical denominations are aware that the Church of the Nazarene does teach that some Christians reach such a spiritual point of commitment that they no longer sin. Some believe that sinlessness is for long periods of time. The book that seemed to have the biggest impact in that movement was *Birthright* by David Needham. Some people understood Needham's book to teach that Christians are so holy once they are in Christ and born again, that they can totally avoid sin; however I did not see that in his book. It was an encouraging book that explained how fully God accepts believers.

A big turning point in my own life came in 1985. I left what had been my most exciting ministry to date in a church in central Arkansas. I had seen God bring genuine revival. It lasted off and on for two years. I left that ministry to come to Memphis to teach at Mid-America Baptist Seminary, where I was responsible to teach church growth, church planting, missions, and spiritual formation. In the fall of 1985, God allowed several events to converge in my life. First, I established a great friendship with one of my colleagues at the seminary. Don and I spent hours eating lunch together and talking about spiritual matters. Talking with Don, it began to dawn on me that God really did accept me. I don't know when the turning point was, but somehow in the friendship and fellowship, God brought an idea to my heart that I was altogether His—that He accepted me like I was, and that I could not do anything to make Him love me more. I began to sing the song "Jesus Loves Me" in a different way. All my life I had sung that song thinking about children, especially little children. In the fall of '85 it seemed appropriate for me to sing "Jesus Loves ME!" Not only did Jesus love children, He loved me just like I was. The song was altogether different now. It was for me; Jesus really loved and accepted me like I was!

That fall I also went to a meeting where Adrian Rogers spoke to a group of ministers. He took Ephesians 1:6 as his text and he used the KJV to read the verse which says, "We are accepted in the beloved." Dr. Rogers emphasized that the verse was saying that we, even those who are ministers, were totally accepted by God. We don't have to wait for His acceptance and for His love. During that devotional talk he emphasized these five truths:

1. God accepts me, that's grace.
2. I accept that He accepts me, that's faith.
3. I accept me, that's peace.
4. Since I accept me, I am free to accept you, that's love.
5. Since I accept you, you are free to accept me, that's fellowship.

I took these truths and wrote them in my Bible and meditated on them many times. They began to make sense to me. It began to occur to me that God really must accept me totally just as I am, and that He doesn't focus mainly on my sin but on His love for me. Previously I had been taught (since High School), that it was essential that I confess my sins to Jesus. 1 John 1:9 says, "If we confess our sins, He is faithful and just to forgive us our sins, and to cleanse us from all unrighteousness." Because of all those years of focusing on my sin so I could stay in fellowship with Jesus, I had developed a sin focus. When I thought of the Lord, I thought of my sin. I desperately wanted to have fellowship with Him, so I thought I had to get rid of all my sin. I found myself almost daily digging with a spiritual shovel in my own heart looking for the sins that might be there—so I could stay in fellowship with the Lord. It dawned on me that I did not have to do this any longer. God loved me totally. He wanted me in fellowship with Him even more than I wanted to be in fellowship with Him. I didn't have to focus on my sin. I could worship Him while I kept an open heart for God to show me my sin.

Now, of course, I still ask Him to show me my sin, but I don't "dig" the same way into my heart. I don't struggle to find any little thing that might be there. I have learned that my loving God will bring to mind those things which will hinder me, those things I must confess. Jude 21 says "Keep yourselves in the love of God" (NKJV). Since I can't hold on to God unless He holds onto me, that verse has to mean that we are to keep ourselves aware of God's love. We are to keep walking with Him so that we will experience His love. As I do, God is true and has been faithful to show me the sin in my life: I want to confess it, and He knows it.

I mentioned earlier that I am privileged to teach a course we call Spiritual Formation. This course is designed to help students learn better how to walk with God and live their life in a devotional manner with regular daily devotional times. In this class I have made it a practice to ask my students these questions, "How many of you would say you sinned over a 100 times yesterday?" I mark down the number of students on the board. "How many of you sinned 50 to a 100 times yesterday?" "How many of you would guess you sinned 25 to 50 times?" "How how many of you sinned 25 times or less yesterday?" I try to make sure everybody responds, and then I look at the board and talk about it with my students. Many of them will say that they probably sinned more than a 100 times yesterday, several more will say 50 to a 100 and so on. A few will say they sinned less than 25 times, but usually it's the smallest category. Then I speak to them and emphasize that sin is rebellion against God. In fact, 1 John3:4 says sin is lawlessness. Of course we commit some sins that we are not actually aware of doing. As believers, however most of the sin we do is conscious, and we are aware of it. Those sins separate us from God and break our fellowship with the Holy Spirit. What I am trying to show my seminary students when I teach this, is that they are loved and accepted by God and are not simply the object of His wrath. Of course God is upset when we deliberately sin, but that is not what their lives consist of regularly.

As I was learning these truths, Romans 8 became the object of my intensive study. Chapter 8 has become my favorite chapter in the entire Bible, and verses 14-17 are probably my favorite verses in this text. Within these verses, there are six word pictures showing how much God loves and accepts us. For instance in verse 14, God calls us "sons of God." Of course, He calls Jesus His son, but in this passage, He calls you and me as Christians the sons of God.

It wasn't until I became a father that I began to see just how truly important this truth was. I was not a daddy until I was 32, and when I became a father this passage and others like it began to speak to my heart in a different way. I have one daughter whom I love deeply. I have gone out of my way to show my love for her. When she was little she loved butterflies, so one day we decided to catch some. On a trip to Florida we had bought a small net which could be used to catch fish and crabs. I thought that it would make a perfect butterfly net. So Meredith and I headed out across our neighborhood and across other people's yards with that net—totally disregarding what other people thought. We were jumping, laughing, and catching butterflies. It was exciting, it was fun, and neither of us cared what was going on in minds of other people. She was only 6 or 7, but I was a grown man, and I was "supposed" to care. However my daughter, my only daughter, wanted me to help her catch butterflies and it just did not matter what others thought. It occurred to me that God feels that way about you and me. He loves and accepts us when others may reject us.

Romans 8:15 states, "You did not receive a spirit that makes you a slave again to fear." "A slave again to fear. . ." It was natural when you and I were not Christians to be totally afraid of God. Just the sheer thought of the great God of the Universe being opposed to us as insignificant individuals was such an awesome thought. We felt that God could do anything to us and would, if He wanted. Then we came to Christ, our lives were changed, we belonged to Jesus, and we were sure of it. The Bible says we are not to be a slave "again to fear." At one time we were, but we are not to be again. We are to be over-comers in the area of fear.

One summer I was visiting some family members, who were avid readers. My sister-in-law loves historical novels. I noticed on one of her shelves that she had the novel *Roots*. I had never read it even though I had seen the miniseries on TV. So I picked up the book and read a chapter. In that chapter Kunta Kinte (the main character) and his fellow slaves, who had been captured in Africa, were brought to America. The mode of travel in those days was ship, so the slaves were put in the bottom, or hold, of the ship where there was little light. There were all kinds of vermin—rats, mice, bugs, and maybe even snakes—in the hold. The slaves were chained in that darkness. The only time that it was light was when the slaves were brought out to the deck of the ship. This could be for punishment or to scrub them down with salt water to help heal the scabs on their bodies. They were scrubbed with rough brushes, and the salt water was mercilessly thrown over their bodies.

The hold would open, light would rush in, and fear would grip the slaves. They knew when the hold was opened they would either be punished or scrubbed down with salt water. Sometimes the punishment for especially rebellious slaves was that their heads would be chopped off with a quick thrust of a sailor's cutlass.

Christians today are not to perceive God as the slaves perceived their mean taskmasters—as punishers of all sorts of wrongs, perceived and real. We can now approach God without fear, with love, and with an awareness of His acceptance.

Romans 8:15 also says that we receive the spirit of adoption (NASB). God has adopted us into His own family. We are not second rate citizens; we are children of the King. Adoption is a very special word. It means that God sought us when we were members of another family, and He adopted us into His family.

Adoption is also special in my family. My wife and I discovered we could not have children when we were 26. In only a few months we had applied for adoption. We wanted to be parents. Quite honestly, the blow and the hurt from this was perhaps the greatest spiritual pain Carol has ever suffered. She had dreamed as a teenager that she might not be able to have children. We had waited until I was almost through seminary before we tried. Then, about the time I graduated, we discovered it was almost impossible.

We applied to adopt a baby at a children's home in New Orleans. It was owned by the Southern Baptist Convention, and its reputation was very good. We waited and waited and waited. Finally we received a call from the agency right before Christmas. This was a hectic season as it was time for us to make our annual trek to our home in Alabama to visit our relatives for the holidays. A staff member from our church and I had stopped off after a Baptist meeting and were shopping at Pete's Shoe Store in North Little Rock, Arkansas when I received a call from Carol. All she could do was cry, and say, "Come home, come home!" We got in the car to come home and I was told that I had another call. I went back to the phone, and she said we had a baby. At the time Carol had the flu, but we were asked to be in New Orleans the next day. So we packed up, and people from our church rallied around us and helped. We left at about eight o'clock that night, drove about eight hours to McComb, Mississippi, and the next morning went to the adoption agency to receive our "package." They brought her out in a Christmas stocking. It was about December 22. They handed her to us in that big, red Christmas stocking, a live package with big bright eyes—the best Christmas gift we ever received.

My daughter is now 28 and married, but she is still the best package I ever got for Christmas. She is adopted, she is loved unconditionally, and we've tried to accept her just like she is. Sometimes we have succeeded with that. All I know is that I'm for adoption—I like it. God adopted me in a similar way. He came looking for me, He paid a price—the life of His only Son. He now loves me just like He loves you.

Romans 8:15 says that we cry to the Lord, "Abba father." Abba is a term of endearment, a term not quite like, but similar to, the word "daddy."

To top it off, the Holy Spirit actually testifies or speaks to our spirit saying that we are God's children (8:16). I have talked to people who say they can't feel the presence of God. They may even doubt that God is still with them. I have realized, because of this verse, that some people who are Christians may feel as if they are not Christians, because verse sixteen is no longer happening in their heart. The Holy Spirit is not testifying with their spirit that they are children of God, because they are not surrendered to the Lordship of Jesus in their lives.

The last picture in this important series of biblical pictures is in verse seventeen. Here God says that since we are children, we are heirs of God and coheirs with Christ (8:17). We all know that being an heir means we have something to inherit. I heard a story about Queen Victoria of England during her childhood days. When she was young, Queen Victoria was said to have been rowdy, rambunctious, and much like a tomboy. At the time she really didn't understand that she would be the next Queen of England. One day one of her nannies was so frustrated with Queen Victoria that she blurted out, "Victoria, a future Queen of England should not act this way!" Suddenly people began to notice a change in the behavior of Victoria. She began to act more Queenly. Someone asked her, "Victoria, what has happened in your life?" and Victoria stated, "You know, some day I will be the Queen of England." When it dawned on Victoria who she was, she began to act differently.

When it dawns on us who we are in Christ, it should make a difference in the way we live and think. Other Bible passages show that God accepts us as we are, loves us totally, and wants us to be comfortable with Him. Romans 8:1 says, "There is now no condemnation for those who are in Christ Jesus." How could it be clearer that God doesn't condemn us when we are in Christ Jesus? Sometimes we allow the world, the flesh, the devil, Christian friends, and our own conscience to condemn us. But, that is not how our Father looks at us. Verse 28 says, "We know that in all things God works for the good of those who love Him." How could God be plainer in His expression of His love and purpose for those of us who are Christians? Please do not read into this that we are not still sinners, and that we do not have to confess our sins. Of course we are, and of course we do. God receives us as children—and He does it with love and acceptance.

At the end of Romans 8, verse 31 says, "If God is for us, who can be against us." Verse 32 states, "He who did not spare His own son, but gave Him up for us all—how will He not also, along with Him, graciously give us all things." Not only is God on our side, not only did He not spare His own son for us, but He promises that He will give us all things which are necessary in our living and service for Him. Jesus is now interceding for us (8:34); this very moment He is praying for you and me. This is the clear teaching of Scripture—He is for us, He is on our side. Verses 38-39 says so convincingly that nothing can separate us from the love of Christ. God even includes in this list "nor anything else in all creation." You and I are included in that statement. We cannot even choose to separate ourselves from the love of God, even if we so desired.

Galatians 4:6-7 almost completely restates those wonderful verses which we talked about in Romans 8:14-17. I am just trying to demonstrate that the truth we have discovered in Ephesians 1:6 and Romans 8:14-17 is not exclusive to those verses. I could go on and on. God is on your side, He loves you totally, and you cannot sin your way away from His love or from His grace. Recently I read in Galatians in my devotions where it says you have fallen from grace. Certainly we can fall away from the grace of God, but we cannot fall out of grace with God. Salvation is a gift. He gave it, and He accepts us in Christ.

In 1971 my wife and I stood at the altar of her home church, and before witnesses and God, we committed to give ourselves only to one another for all of our lives. We have been true to that commitment. Along the way we have found fault with one another. We have found areas where we were not compatible, and we've even had strong disagreements over some of these areas. However we haven't and we never will reject each other because of our disagreements. How I wish that all God's children could understand that HE will never reject us either!

# 9

# COMMITTED CHRISTIANS

## *The Devotional Life*

I CAN'T REMEMBER when I first heard about "having a quiet time." I must have been a teenager, because I have heard the term so many times now. Other people talk about having personal devotions, having time with God, spending time alone with God, and even manna in the morning. It does not really matter what we call our time with God, what really matters is that we have some. The big problem here is that there are many sincere Christians who just cannot seem to establish a time with God.

Walt Henrickson wrote an insightful book called *Disciples Are Made Not Born*. Someone gave me a tape of Henrickson speaking to a group of Navigator leaders; if you are not familiar with the Navigators, I feel that they are one of the most committed groups of Christians that work on college campuses. Hendrickson himself was a Navigator when he wrote this book. I am not sure of the size of the group, but the background noises suggest it was fifty to a hundred people. It was a small group, but it was an important group in the Christian world. Hendrickson was funny and profound and at the end of the tape he was very pointed to this extremely committed group of Christian leaders. He said that he believed that only about ten of them would be going on for God and seriously serving Jesus in about a decade. What a frightening thought!

Why does this kind of fallout occur? It happens because people get away from God in their heart. How does that happen? That happens, perhaps more often than not, because people quit spending regular time with God. It's hard to spend time alone with Jesus and not have a surrendered heart toward Him. It is hard to spend time with Jesus and be in open sin. It is just hard to spend time with Jesus alone and not try to walk with Him in a sincere way. When we lose the habit of spending time with the Lord on a regular basis, we are likely to slip away from Him as our Lord.

I entered the gospel ministry when I was 21 and in college. I had surrendered to the ministry when I was 20 during the very middle of the Jesus movement. I was a student at the University of Alabama and my future wife and I began to attend Christian functions on campus, and we began to grow. From this point until the time I was 23 and first beginning seminary, I read the

Bible, prayed, and studied the Bible, but my devotional habits were not regular. There was not a steadiness about my time with God. In the fall of my first year in seminary, something just clicked in my heart, and I determined that I must spend time with the Lord Jesus every day. At that point in 1974, I began a devotional habit which continues to this day in 2011. Certainly I have missed some days when I did not have a time with God, but there have not been many days. I am grateful to say that the habit is firmly established, no matter what happens in my life, and I'm committed to continue the practice.

Now, I am no example, but everyone must come to a commitment when they determine that no matter what happens they will spend time alone with the Lord. You can call it what you wish, you can do it in your own way, but if you are going to go on with God, you simply must establish this routine.

It's interesting to think about how many Christians in our country do spend time regularly and daily with God. One of my joys in teaching at a seminary is that I'm allowed to teach a course called Spiritual Formation, as I mentioned earlier. This is the class were students are supposed to learn how to have a time with God. I decided one year to find out how many of them were already having time with God—before they got to the class. I did a simple survey. I asked them not to put any names on the paper but on a small piece of paper to write 1 sentence with two blanks: "I spend about ____ minutes per day on _____ days per week." This was a short and sweet survey, but it helped someone in my position determine where his students were. I have kept some of these questionnaires, and I would estimate that my typical student spends about fifteen to twenty minutes a day about 3 or 4 days per week. Many of these seminary students are in their first year. Many of them have not established solid Christian habits yet. Also, keep in mind that these students are the "best of the best." As a whole they are very sincere Christians that have a heart for God. They try to share their faith, and most of them win people to Jesus Christ. In this group of the "best of the best," the average student among them is not spending much time with Christ in a given week.

I'm not trying to cast guilt on you, the reader. I know what it is like to be struggling with the devotional habit, and I also know that guilt usually won't do much to motivate you and me in the long term.

Of course the Bible talks about spending time alone with God. In Mark 1:35 Scripture talks about Jesus very early in His ministry rising early in the morning and getting alone with His Father. His is the best example we will ever have. The Son, who knew He was the Son of God, chose to spend time with His Father. He was also equal with God. The creator of the world (Col. 1) chose to submit Himself to His heavenly Father and spend time with Him. Paul, the great church planter and apostle spent lots of time with his Lord. At the end of his life, he told Timothy in II Timothy 4:13, "When you come, bring the cloak. . . and my scrolls especially the parchments." Paul had much time on his hands, and he enjoyed praying in the prison, but he also wanted the Word of God as contained on the scrolls and parchments. As you read through Paul's letters over and over you get the impression that Paul had been in prayer, and He had been studying the Word of God.

Lately for my quiet time I have been in the book of Ezekiel. I've been through Ezekiel many times now, but this time it seems to be speaking to me more than ever. Ezekiel, one of the main prophets in the Old Testament, wrote a rather long book—containing 48 chapters. Within the book there is prophesy, and also a good amount of exhortation and rebuke to the nation of Israel. The early part of Ezekiel reveals that Ezekiel spent time alone with God. In Ezekiel 1:3 he said, "The word of the Lord came to Ezekiel..." Certainly Ezekiel was alone with God when this occurred; he was spending time with God. In Ezekiel 2:1 we read, "He said to me, "Son of man, stand up on your feet and I will speak to you." We can only imagine what posture Ezekiel was in before God said to him, "Stand up," but here Ezekiel is apparently alone with God, and God tells him to rise to his feet. In Ezekiel 3:1, Ezekiel is alone with God and God tells him to eat a certain scroll. This may seem like a strange request, but God is not in a box, and He may not act like we expect Him to. Ezekiel was literally to eat the scroll. The point is that Ezekiel was alone with God when He told him this very important command. Ezekiel 3:12 says, "Then the Spirit lifted me up, and I heard behind me a loud rumbling sound—

May the glory of the Lord be praised in his dwelling place!" Ezekiel was alone and worshiping God when the Spirit lifted him up, and he heard this loud rumbling sound.

The point about Ezekiel is this—he spent much time alone with God. As a result God spoke to him and gave him private instruction. In Ezekiel 1:3, Scripture says that the word of the Lord came to Ezekiel by the Kebar River. Obviously Ezekiel was alone and outside by the river with God. I cannot emphasize enough how important it is for Christians to spend time alone in nature with God—not worshiping nature but worshiping God in His creation.

## Getting Started

WHY IS IT SO difficult to get started having a time alone with God? It was hard for me to get started, and I have known many others who have had a hard time in the beginning maintaining a regular quiet time.

Perhaps it will help us if we realize the benefit of having a regular time with God, and the consequences if we do not. First, what does it do for us if we have a regular time with God? In John 10:3-4 Jesus said that His sheep hear His voice. It is difficult to hear the voice of Jesus with the world's noise pounding in our ears. When we get alone with Him, we will hear His voice. Additionally, it helps us to learn and apply the

Bible to our lives. There is nothing more important in the life of a believer than the Word of God. Most evangelical Christians would agree with that, although the majority of those same Christians probably do not spend regular time in the Bible. They revere the Bible and believe it, but they have a hard time becoming regular readers of it. But if we do become constant readers and students of the Word of God, we begin to get a feel for it, and we begin to hear His voice more readily. This normally means that we hear His voice in the very words of Scripture as God often speaks through the Bible.

If we spend time with God it helps us to grow as believers. Not many things in the Christian realm are sadder than to know someone who has been saved for decades but is still a baby Christian. Some people would say that it's the churches' fault that he is still a baby Christian. Of course the church contributes to this, but the church is not mainly at fault. That baby Christian is mainly at fault, as he has not spent time with God on his own. Another benefit of spending regular time with God is that our prayer life begins it grow. Many people find it difficult to pray more than just a short prayer. As we spend time with the Lord and practice prayer, we grow in our understanding and feel of how to pray and what to pray for. Of course this leads us to experience closeness with our Lord. By this I mean that we can sense His presence in our life.

Recently I was sitting in my backyard where we have some beautiful flowers and trees. My wife had been drinking coffee with me, but she went inside, and I was there alone. I began to sense the presence of God in a strong way, so I meditated on the Lord and cherished the moment as God's presence bathed me in His love. This kind of thing happens to me occasionally and sometimes regularly, but might not, if I were not practicing the habit of spending time with Jesus daily. So, a quiet time gives us time to love God and for Him to love us back. Jude 21 says, "Keep yourselves in God's love..." I have thought a good bit about that verse, as I said earlier, and the only meaning I can come up with is that God is saying to keep ourselves aware of His love, and to keep reminding ourselves that He loves us. Since it's obvious that we cannot keep ourselves in God's love on our own, we must continually stay aware that He loves us.

An additional benefit of spending time alone with God is that as we draw near to Him, the Holy Spirit is faithful to show us when sin is in our life. 1 John 1:8 says, "If we claim to be without sin we deceive ourselves…" All of us have sinned and we all sin regularly. When we spend time with Jesus personally, He shows us our sin specifically, and we are able to stay clean from it. Another benefit of spending regular time with God is that when you do it you don't feel guilty that you haven't done it. It has been so popular to talk about a quiet time in the last few decades that most Christians know that they should spend time with God, and they simply go on feeling guilty. When you spend time with the Lord you don't have to feel guilty that you have not.

I like to tell the story of my first year in college, when my wife Carol and I were in different colleges. She was at the University of Alabama, and I was at Jacksonville State University in northeastern Alabama, about three hours away. We kept up with the weekends that we did not see one another that first year, and there were only two. I would go to her college or she would come to mine or we would meet in our home town. We were in love, and there was a growing commitment to one another. So when we were separated by what seemed like a great distance we would write letters to each other. In fact during the week every day we would write a letter to one another, and it just became a habit. They were not long, they were just mushy and reminded us that we genuinely loved each other and were committed to one another. At this time I was living in a boys' dormitory named Dixon Hall. I would walk into Dixon after letter time and I would see the post office boxes that we all had and I would pass them up. I would go to my room and take a nap or go out and play sports with the guys. Later that night I would probably remember that I had a letter from Carol, my love. So I would drag myself down to get the letter, smell of it (sometimes it smelled like perfume), and I would drag myself back to my dorm room and fall asleep for the evening. The next day I would think, "I have to write her a letter so I better read what she said." So I would take that letter to class sometime during class I would rip it open quietly and sit there and read the letter during the lecture. Sometimes I would finish the letter during one class, sometimes it would take me two, since they were about a page long.

Now if you believe that's the way I acted toward her letters, then I would like to interest you in some beach front property in Kansas! Of course that's not the way I treated her love letters. I would know the time when letters would be put up, and sometimes I would open my box and be standing there when a letter would be put into my box. I would almost reach out and grab it from the hand of the letter handler. Then I would smell it right there and rip it open, and sometimes I would read that letter right on the spot, right in front of the boxes and in the way of everybody else. I was in love! I would take the letter to class with me and read it again during class over, and over, and think about it, and smell it, and dream of the weekend when I would once again be with Carol. You see, when there is true love, people act differently.

I want to remind you that this is Jesus we are talking about. He really loves you. He wants to spend time with you, and He wants you to want to spend time with Him. So somehow in the near future, if you are not having a daily time with God, you must change that.

Now let's think about this issue from the other side. What does it do for us as Christians if we do not spend regular daily time with God? I would venture to say that among active, serious, committed Christians, half of us still do not spend daily time with God—at least half. What does it do for those of us who are trying to be committed Christians, and we don't spend regular time with God? First, we will experience guilt in our lives. God doesn't want us to live with guilt, but if we don't spend time alone with the Lord, and read the Word and pray, we will feel guilty. Also we will begin to drift away from the Lord spiritually if we don't spend regular time with Him. I have recently gone through the book of Acts, and it's quite a story that I love to hear over and over.

In the last few chapters of Acts, Paul was being taken to Rome because he had appealed to Caesar over the terrible treatment he was receiving. The Roman authorities put him on an Alexandrian ship, and they headed west toward the great city of Rome. It was getting late in the season and the danger for storms was high. The Captain of the ship was warned that they should winter at Fair Havens but he stubbornly chose to go on. They got a good wind and headed in the direction of Rome, when all of a sudden a northeaster came out of nowhere. Before the storm was over, (almost two weeks later) the captain and the officers of the ship had decided to drop anchor and simply let the ship be blown where it would. This was a dangerous choice, but it is about the only choice they had. The wind howled and blew, and the ship simply drifted and faced danger after danger. Many Christians live their spiritual lives this way. They drop anchor and simply drift, going in no particular direction. These people still go to church; they still try to avoid obvious sin, however they are just drifting. I have done it, you have done it, and we know what it is like. If you spend regular daily time with God this is not as likely to happen.

Additionally, if we avoid spending time with God, sin will begin to build up in our lives. It is harder to see sin in our lives if we are not bringing our life into the light of God Himself. If we get in the light the light will reveal wrongs in our life. If we avoid spending time with God, we are not learning from the Bible. We are not regularly spending time in prayer. We're much more likely to stay surrendered to Jesus as our Lord on a daily basis if we spend time with Him, in the Bible and in prayer. In fact it's rather hard to imagine spending time with Christ daily and not having a desire to be surrendered to Him.

When I was in seminary, one of my favorite preachers was Peter Lord. He was a pastor in Florida, and he was also best friends with Adrian Rogers (my favorite preacher). During my second year of seminary, Peter Lord came to a church in Memphis and held a conference on the Christian life. I only went once, but what I heard was eye opening. Peter had done a survey at this church a couple of nights earlier asking those in attendance how many of them had a daily time with God. It's important to know that this was a strong church, that was very evangelistic, and the spirit of revival was on the church. He asked them about their devotional life. He revealed to us the night I was present that the survey showed in that very good church, of the Monday or Tuesday crowd (the committed crowd), that about half of them spent time regularly with God. I was shocked! What if this same survey was done on Sunday morning? Would it be less than 25%? I think it would, and I think it probably would be in your church as well. Perhaps less than 25% of the active members of your church have a daily quiet time! Remember, that is not to cast guilt, that is to say that you and I can be different. I know you've probably made commitments to change this situation in your life over, and over, during a conference or a revival meeting at your church. You have probably gone to the altar, prayed, wept and begged God to help you develop a daily time with Him, and then you failed again. I'm not asking you to do that, I'm just trying to show you that the most important thing you could do in your Christian life would be to establish a daily quiet time.

## What Does it Look Like?

I THINK SOME PEOPLE may be thinking, "What does it consist of, this important time you have with God?" Let me describe a typical time that I spend with God. Now remember, I am different. I don't do everything in the expected manner, I'm not very orthodox, but here goes. On a typical day I will spend about 20 to 25 minutes listening to the Bible. I have the Bible in the NIV version, and I have the Old and New Testament. Yesterday I went to my favorite park which is 4 or 5 minutes from my house to have my time with God. I sat in my car parked under a tree for shade, since it is summer now in the Memphis area. I sat there and probably listened to 5 or 6 chapters in the Bible. At this point in time I am listening to the Book of Proverbs and the Book of Matthew, so I listen some to each book. Along the way I paused my CD player when I came to something that struck me as significant, or it just spoke to my heart.

I will pause my CD player and think on a passage or maybe pray over an issue that the Bible has brought to my attention. Nothing is too small to notice when it comes to God's Word. After I have pondered this particular detail or truth I will turn my CD player on again and continue to listen, praying occasionally as I go through the Bible. After I have listened to a few chapters—no particular number, I am free in that I listen to as much as I wish—I will turn to a time of prayer. I did this yesterday. I began to pray for people in my life, starting with those who are close to me, my family, people I work with, my neighbors. I have neighbors who are not Christians and I have a relationship with several of them, so I pray for them regularly. I honestly plan to win some of them to Christ. Then I pray for a few more things. My prayer time yesterday probably lasted 12 to 15 minutes, but that's 12 to 15 minutes in addition to the time I spent in prayer during my Bible time. After a few minutes of praying, I surrendered myself that day and my body a living sacrifice to Jesus (Romans 12:1). This is a routine I have, but it is a good one. I tell God that I surrender. I tell Him (according to Romans 6:6) that I know that I am dead unto sin, and that sin will no longer reign over me. I reckon that I'm dead as I'm told to do in Romans 6:11. Reckon means to count or consider it to be done. So I reckon myself to be dead. Then I ask God to show me any sin in my life. I try not to linger here long— just as long as I am seeing sin. One of the truths of 1 John 1:9 is that we can confess sin any time—we don't have to wait for our quiet time. So I confess any sin, I've already surrendered my heart, and at this point I boldly ask the Holy Spirit to control me, to fill me. Then I go through the 6 pieces of armor in Ephesians 6, and I pray through the armor of God in relation to me.

This is what I do with God on a regular basis. Sometimes I change it, sometimes on occasion I will read in a devotional book. Right now I'm reading Dr. Bill Bright's last book *The Journey Home*, which was finished 2 or 3 weeks before he died. It has been rich, and I don't consider it to be Scripture, but to be a devotional book which challenges my heart. This is not a pattern that you need to copy, but if you have no pattern I will loan it to you for awhile until you establish your own. The point is, we should daily spend some time with God. By the way, recently while I was in the park in my car spending time praying, I fell asleep. For 10 or 15 minutes I slept "before the Lord!" Now, that did not take away from my quiet time, in fact I think it added to it. I awoke refreshed, spent more time with God, and I was ready to go. The point is we can be free with Jesus if we are surrendered to Him, in the Word of God, and trying to do His will. There is a freedom to be yourself as you serve Him.

I could add a large number of suggestions to make the devotional life have variety. If you are interested in some of the more classic approaches to spending time with God, check out Richard Foster's book *Celebration of Discipline*. Foster is a Quaker, so some of the ideas are going to be different if you are not a Quaker. However this book has become the classic when it comes to examining the spiritual disciplines. I would definitely add the reading of devotional literature as a part of a quiet time. Remember most of the reading you do during a devotional time should be the Bible.

After you have done your Bible reading and prayer time and have some more time to spend with the Lord, reading a devotional book can be extremely helpful. I'll recommend a few books and authors. Watchman Nee and Jack Taylor are the most unique devotional writers I have ever read. Both of them come up with spiritual ideas that seem to have never been pondered by anyone. Jack Taylor wrote *The Key to Triumphant Living* in 1971. This book was a huge hit and opened many (particularly Southern Baptists) to the idea of being filled with the Holy Spirit. Billy Graham has written several books which are devotional in nature. His book *The Holy Spirit* is an excellent study of the Holy Spirit and is good for committed Christians. The works of Vance Havner—he wrote about 40 books—are excellent devotional literature.

Havner died in the 80's, but he was a powerful Baptist evangelist that God used widely. Max Lucado, with books like *No Wonder They Call Him the Savior* has been a favorite devotional writer of many people for almost two decades. Lucado can describe Jesus' death on the cross like nobody ever could in my opinion. All of these are what I consider devotional books. They are good reading for part of your quiet time.

You may choose to listen to the Bible, read the Bible, or have somebody read the Bible to you, but just make sure you take in Scripture. Christian music is also a great part of the devotional life for many people, and I recommend it, but I recommend it with caution. Don't let music become your Bible; use it as a small part of your quiet time. Remember we are free in Christ, but make sure you spend time in the word of God.

Christians should spend time alone with God in nature. Find a place where you can be in the woods with God. Your prayer life may take on a new direction. You can pray standing, walking, driving, on your knees, or lying down. When I first started teaching at the seminary, I did a revival meeting in a church in Mississippi, and I stayed with an older couple. They showed me their prayer closet which contained a chair and that was all. It was literally a small closet where they would go and be alone with God. Now, that's not for me, because I'm an outside boy, but it may be for you. I asked my daughter about her devotional time and she said that she had about a 30 minute break on her job, and she took her devotional materials and did her quiet time there. You can spend time with God just about anywhere; just make sure it includes the Word of God and prayer.

I don't spend a lot of time on vacation in a normal year, but I do spend some. I have learned to spend time with the Lord on vacation. I have to find somewhere special to get alone. That place is usually my automobile. I have learned to spend time with God in my car. When we were in Gulf Shores, Alabama one year I found a state park very close by. It had some inland water, was a natural habitat for birds and animals, and it was a great place to spend time with the Lord. We don't have to backslide on our vacation, we can find a place to spend time with God. When I miss spending time in the morning (my normal habit) I have learned that I can find time at work, or in the afternoon after work to spend with Jesus. It doesn't have to legalistically be done in the morning as some people will make you think. You can spend time with Jesus anytime. I have a good friend whom I have known for 36 years, and his habit is to spend time with God at night. He just does not like getting up in the morning. He has a hard time sleeping, so he spends time at night with the Lord Jesus.

## Barriers

A HUGE BARRIER TO people spending time with God is their feelings. Sometimes more often than not you won't feel like spending time with God. I can testify that if you will keep doing it there will come a time when feelings just don't matter much. You learn to do it because you know it's important, and because you know that God wants to meet with you. Honestly, sometimes I spend time with the Lord so I won't feel guilty that I haven't done so. Now that doesn't seem like a good motive, but in the midst of the time with God, He will capture my attention and my heart and my motives will change. The devil himself wants to keep you away from a regular quiet time. We could say the first and biggest barrier to a daily quiet time is Satan. He will make sure things happen in your life which will distract you. They may seem small and not so evil, but they distract you from having time with God. If Jesus is your first priority, of course Satan wants to keep you away from Him. There are many barriers that I could mention which will keep you from your time with God. Probably the most obvious barrier is business—overwork. When you get too busy, one of the quickest things to go is usually spending time with God.

I talked to a pastor about a staff position back in college, and on one occasion I dropped by his house and spoke to his wife. She told me her husband was working 16 hours a day and loving it. Honestly it scared me a little, because I wondered if he would expect me to work like that. I wound up not taking the staff position that was offered to me, but I also wondered about that pastor who was supposedly spending 16 hours a day serving the Lord. How in the world did he carve out time to spend with the Lord and with his family—our first two priorities?

A very simple barrier to spending time with God is sin in our lives. I doubt that King David spent much time in prayer and doing the holy things of God (including reading his Bible) during his 9 months of rebellion after his incident with Bathsheba. I doubt that many of us would do any differently.

Spiritual dryness can be a barrier to spending time with God. Dryness is when we just cannot sense or feel the presence of God. We read the Bible and no bells or whistles go off. We pray and it seems as if our prayers stay in the room. Our desire to share Christ and to do good for others seems to be gone. First, let me warn you that dryness in your Christian walk can lead to discouragement, so be careful about that transition. Spiritual dryness will come. There will be times when you will not feel holy. Try to ignore those feelings and just keep plowing on for Jesus. Isaiah 50 discusses this particular issue. In 50:10 Isaiah asks, "Who fears the Lord and yet walks in the dark and has no light." What does he advise us to do? In verse 10 he says to trust in the name of the Lord and rely on his God. In other words keep trusting God, keep leaning on Jesus. Verse 11 is a warning that those who are in the dark should not light their own fire. If we do, we may "lie down in torment." So if we are not to light our own fire, we are to wait and allow the Lord to light our fire again. We have all heard the expression of those who are "on fire for God." Even those who are on fire for God have times when they don't feel like it. I have been there and you have too. So keep trusting God and doing what is right in the middle of difficult and dry times.

If we are not totally committed to a time alone with God on a daily basis, it will not happen. It may happen initially for two or three weeks even, but we just won't continue if we do not have a firm commitment to a time with God.

Debt can also keep us from spending time with God. You may wonder, how? When we are in debt, we Christians tend to want to get out of debt. We take another job, we work harder, and we are not able to spend time with God or with our family. It is difficult to serve God through our church, because we work all the time. Someone has said, "A man has the right to earn all the money he can as long as he does it honestly." The only problem with that statement is that it is just not true. While we are earning all the money we can, we are breaking the priorities that God has given us. This applies to debt and the life of the Christian. I know of a very committed Christian who has three jobs, is taking courses in higher education, has a family, and is serving in his church. There is only so much time in a day and someone has said that Jesus never got in a hurry to do anything.

How in the world can the man I know have time for the Lord and his family?

There are certainly other barriers to spending time with God, but these should suffice for us to say that if you're not committed totally to Christ and to a quiet time, you just won't have one. It's a matter of priorities.

Many committed Christians don't make it a priority to spend time with God on a daily basis. Thank God many do and they practice what they believe. I may be talking to you. If you have toyed with the idea and the practice of a daily quiet time and still have not conquered this area of your Christian life, it is time for another go at it. It is time for you to win this battle. God will give you the power to do so if you are totally submitted to Him, full of His Spirit. Make it a priority now to begin spending time every day with the Lord. Start short. Ten minutes is a good start, but start, and God will bless you for it.

# 10

# THE KEY

## *To the Christian Life*

---

IF YOU WERE AN active Christian in the 1970s, you may know the name Jack Taylor. Taylor is a Baptist minister, and at that time he was the pastor of First Baptist Church Castle Hills in San Antonio, Texas. He wrote a book called *The Key to Triumphant Living*. In that book he discussed how he had discovered that Colossians 1:27 contained the key to the Christian life. It states, "Which is Christ in you, the hope of glory" (NKJV). Jack Taylor had learned during the previous decade that he could not live the Christian life on his own. In fact he was a failure if he tried. He discovered that Jesus actually lived in him daily and that he needed to be controlled by the Spirit of God—in other words he needed to be filled with the Holy Spirit. In the book he talks about his journey in discovering these things, and what took place in his church when he preached these truths. In a nutshell, revival broke out at Castle Hills First Baptist Church.

These were the days of the Jesus movement, or the Jesus revolution. God was moving in many places and in many churches, especially among young people. Jerry Glisson was the pastor of Leawood Baptist Church here in Memphis. About 1970 Glisson learned about being filled with the Spirit, and part of it he learned from Jack Taylor. Glisson wrote a book called *The Church in a Storm*. When Glisson began to preach about being filled with the Spirit, revival also broke out in his church. As God would have it Glission was the president of the Tennessee Baptist Convention that same year and when he brought the President's address at the Tennessee Baptist Convention, he preached on being filled with the Spirit—a bold move in 1970.

Up until this time many evangelicals (including Baptists) did not speak much about the Holy Spirit and especially about being filled with the Holy Spirit. Jack Taylor became the number one selling author for Southern Baptist's Broadman Press, and his message on the Spirit-filled life was spread widely. By the end of the 70s, Baptists talked rather openly about being filled with the Holy Spirit. In the early 1980s some factors occurred which seemed to put the brakes on this open discussion about the Holy Spirit. In the decades since the 1980s, this "fear" of the Holy Spirit has remained in far too many of our churches and in Christian circles. Today there is a lack of preaching and teaching on the Holy Spirit Himself and especially on the filling of the Holy Spirit. This lack is all the more puzzling in light of the fact that the filling of the Holy Spirit is the key to the Christian life. How can anyone serve the Lord without the power of the Lord? The means to obtain the power is through the filling of the Holy Spirit.

Several years ago I was teaching a "Spiritual Formation" class at our seminary. One day a student named Tim came to my office and poured his heart out to me. He shared how he was not experiencing joy in his Christian life, how all the other students were thrilled by the teaching they were receiving, but he was just not sharing that joy. I shared some thoughts with him, prayed for him, and sent him on his way. A few weeks later he came back to me in private, and he was just glowing. A big smile was on his face, and he was obviously different. I wanted to know why, so we began to talk about what had happened. He shared with me how one night at home he had picked up Bill Bright's little booklet, *Have You Made the Wonderful Discovery of the Spirit Filled Life*. This booklet contains the basic teaching on how to be filled with the Spirit. Tim had read the booklet and was so excited about what it taught that he read the booklet again with his wife. Then both of them prayed asking the Lord to control their life and fill them both with the Holy Spirit. Tim shared with me how Jesus had changed him since that evening, and how joy had come into his life. Today I require all of my classes, including PhD students, to read the same booklet by Bill Bright on how to be filled with the Holy Spirit. Even students who earn their Doctorate here at our fine biblical seminary are deliberately taught how to be controlled by the Spirit, otherwise they may not learn how.

My own encounter with the Holy Spirit began back in 1967, the year I became a Christian. At youth camp at Panama City, Florida, my pastor was teaching a study to our church's youth group, and he began to talk about the Holy Spirit. I remember distinctly asking him some basic questions about the Holy Spirit, such as "Is there really a Holy Spirit? I have not heard of Him." I was that ignorant of the Holy Spirit, and I had been in Christian churches most of my life. That next year I encountered teaching on the filling of the Holy Spirit through the same booklet that I require my students to read today—Bill Bright's booklet, *Have You Made the Wonderful Discovery of the Spirit Filled Life.* Through Bright's booklet I made that wonderful discovery! What had been foggy in my mind had now become clear. I understood what it was to walk with the Spirit of God. This all took place before Jack Taylor wrote his book *The Key to Triumphant Living* and before many Christians in America were talking openly about the filling of the Spirit. Of all people I was most privileged! God was working in my life in a wonderful way, and the key was my relationship with the Spirit of God, and the Lord Jesus.

The first time I ever remember hearing someone verbally explain the filling of the Spirit was on a Sunday afternoon around April of my junior year of High School. We were having a major youth-led evangelistic crusade, and I had volunteered to be a counselor. The training for counselors took place on a Sunday afternoon at the YMCA in my hometown. There were about 100 young people being trained by Carl Wilson, the National High School Director for Campus Crusade for Christ's High School Ministry. Most of what Wilson told us had to do with spiritual matters, not with details concerning counseling. He took us to John 7 where Jesus spoke at the Feast of the Tabernacles, and he told us that this passage contained what was most important for counselors at an evangelistic crusade. First he said we must be hungry and thirsty Christians (v. 37). Then we must come to Christ in full surrender, Jesus said "Let him come to me." Then we must ask God to do what He wants us to. We must ask him to fill us with His Spirit. Verse 38 involves the faith which is required for someone to be controlled by God's Spirit, and then the end of verse 38 shows the results—rivers of living water flowing out of us.

After Carl Wilson had shown us some of these truths, he asked us to bow our heads, and close our eyes. I remember this so clearly—it was life changing. I was sitting in the back right section of the group, when Wilson asked us to pray and ask the Holy Spirit to control our lives. He then asked us to raise our hands if we had prayed with him. I had a bird's eye view of most of the group, so I covered my eyes and then peeked through my hands and saw that almost every hand in the room was raised. My hand was raised, also. What a great discovery for a young Christian, or for any Christian. God's desire is to fill us and control us for His glory. I was on my way to learning how to be a Spirit-filled Christian.

This is the key to living for God. We are told to worship in the Spirit in John 4. We are told to pray in the Spirit in Ephesians 6. We are told that we will have power to witness after the Holy Spirit comes to us in Acts 1:8. The Holy Spirit and His filling in our life is essential if we are going to serve God.

## What Does the Bible Have to Say About Him?

EARLY IN THE OLD TESTAMENT it becomes obvious that being filled with the Holy Spirit is essential for Christian service. Bezalel and Oholiab, who worked on the tabernacle, were filled with the Holy Spirit. Obviously, God even wants His craftsmen who are doing work for Him to be filled with the Spirit. The Lord Jesus Christ began His ministry with a trip into the wilderness to be tempted by the devil. The Bible states that He was filled with the Holy Spirit when He went into the wilderness, and that He came out of the wilderness in the power of the Holy Spirit. Luke 4:1 says, "Then Jesus, being filled with the Holy Spirit, returned from the Jordan and was led by the Spirit into the wilderness" (NKJV). If Jesus was filled with the Holy Spirit, certainly we must be controlled by the Holy Spirit. Luke 3:14 says, "Then Jesus returned in the power of the Spirit to Galilee" (NKJV). The Holy Spirit and His filling were key in the ministry of our Lord Jesus Christ.

Acts 2 recounts that the Holy Spirit came on the day of Pentecost, and all believers who were gathered together were filled with the Holy Spirit. This means that Simon (Big Mouth) Peter was filled with the Holy Spirit. The lives of the Apostles demonstrate a dramatic change after Acts 2. Before the day of Pentecost, the Apostles were weak and powerless believers. After the day of Pentecost, the Bible reveals them as different, powerful men. They had the power of God, the Holy Spirit working in their life.

Today there is a good bit of teaching and preaching about the Holy Spirit, His person, His work, etc. I listen closely at the end of this kind of teaching and many Christian speakers will not talk about *how to be filled with the Holy Spirit.* We are told in Scripture to do so, so surely there's a way for this to occur in our lives.

The main character in most of the New Testament is the Apostle Paul. If you examine his life, you will find how important the Holy Spirit was to him. He talked freely about being filled with the Spirit and walking in the Spirit (Ephesians 5, Galatians 5).

Some people teach that all Christians are filled with the Holy Spirit since all Christians have the Holy Spirit in them. The last part of their argument is true—the Holy Spirit does reside in the heart of every true believer. Not every believer, however, is filled with the Holy Spirit, otherwise why would we be commanded in God's Word to be filled with the Holy Spirit? In Ephesians 5:18 we are directly commanded to be filled with the Spirit. This book was written to believers who lived in Ephesus. Obviously some of the believers were filled with the Spirit, and some were not.

## What the Filling of the Spirit Ain't

PEOPLE HAVE STRANGE ideas about what it means to be filled with the Holy Spirit. This section examines some significant themes, but many ideas are omitted. As I mentioned above, every Christian is not controlled by the Holy Spirit, yet God wants all Christians to be filled with the Spirit. Several ideas have been used by the enemy to turn us away from the truth of the Spirit filled life.

First, the filling of the Spirit ain't avoiding stuff. Every community seems to have its own list of taboos that Christians can't indulge in. You will usually find that whiskey, tobacco, gambling, cursing, sexual immorality, and R and X rated movies are on this list. It is just about universal. Some communities, however, add other things to the list of stuff that must be avoided if you're going to be a good Christian—in other words if you are going to be a Spiritual Christian.

When I was a boy, about 12 years old, I was visiting with a friend of mine whose name was Randy. His father was a good man, but he was narrow in his views. The family had a nice home and a big living room with nice carpet, and one day Randy and I were in the carpeted living room throwing playing cards at a hat. We were having a good time seeing who could get the most cards in the hat. Randy's father walked through and saw what we were doing. I remember his anger and even some of his words. He told us that if we did this kind of thing, before long we'd be gambling and really going against what God wanted us to do. So, I guess in some communities you can put throwing cards at a hat on your list of taboo things that cannot be done by Christians. You get the idea. I am not implying that it's okay to drink whiskey, etc. . . . Certainly those things which are biblically prohibited should be avoided by all Christians by all means. However, avoiding doing things will not make you a spiritual Christian. It just makes you a Christian who has avoided stuff. Avoidance of sin will not get you filled you with the Holy Spirit.

Second, the filling of the Holy Spirit doesn't occur by comparing ourselves with other Christians. It seems to bring great joy to some Christians to observe that other Christians who are considered to be really good Christians do certain things which just shouldn't be done. These believers compare themselves with the other Christians and feel like they are more spiritual than the other believers.

Peter, James, and John were taken to the Mount of Transfiguration with Jesus. They saw Jesus transfigured before their very eyes, and they observed Moses and Elijah talking with Jesus. Have you ever wondered how Simon Peter knew it was Moses and Elijah? You can imagine what a "heady" experience this was for those three disciples. They came down the mountain just glowing with joy, and then they encountered the other nine disciples. I can't help but wonder if Peter, James, and John didn't feel like they were just a little more spiritual than the other nine disciples because they had had this experience.

The Pharisees had a habit of acting like they were "more spiritual." In Luke 18:11-13, Jesus talked about the Pharisee who compared himself to other men who were sinners. Jesus certainly was not saying that it was okay to do what this sinner had done, but he was teaching us that it doesn't make us spiritual when we compare ourselves with other believers.

Third, we are not filled with the Holy Spirit by our own discipline. Bill Bright used to talk about a man he had known who had a little black book in which he wrote down everything he was supposed to do—all his jobs, etc. He appeared to be an extremely disciplined man. That is until he almost had a breakdown. He was not able to make himself good on his own.

He looked spiritual on the outside, but he almost was broken over it.

One of the best things we can do is to read our Bible and spend time with God. It‘s a daily practice of mine, and I recommend it for everyone. Reading the Bible daily and praying does not mean we are controlled by the Holy Spirit. This truth in no way belittles discipline; it simply affirms that discipline alone does not equal the Spirit's filling. It is wonderful to have habits that are spiritual and godly. It is good to have routines which help you walk with God. They just don't make you spiritual in themselves.

Fourth, we are not filled with the Holy Spirit because of our emotions, and our emotional experiences. Please don't take me wrong, I am for good godly emotions. On occasion I cry, sometimes I shout to the Lord in private, I lift my hands (although it is usually in private), and I also regularly feel the presence of God in my life. I'm not criticizing any of these things. I'm just saying emotions do not equal the filling of the Spirit.

Billy Graham tells a story about a man who was not a Christian, who went forward in a Christian service to "the mourners' bench." While he was there on his knees, a faithful Christian came up and knelt down beside him and said, "Hold on brother you've got to hold on to find the Lord." Another good Christian who meant well came up to the mourners' bench and whispered in the brothers ear, "Let go brother, you got to let go to give your life to God." A third well meaning Christian came and knelt beside the brother, "Look for a bright light, I saw a bright light when I was saved." Well the man was saved and later he was testifying and he said this, "Between trying to hold on, let go, and look for that bright light, I almost didn't make it."

Those three well-meaning believers were simply sharing what they had experienced, and how emotions had moved them when they were saved. They meant well, but emotions do not make you spiritual. Emotions are good, some are actually God given, but they are no substitute for surrender, holiness, and being filled with the Holy Spirit.

I hope you get the point. People have come up with many ways to make themselves spiritual. I could add other things to this list like praying "enough," or crucifying yourself. But I think the most often used strategy by Christians to make themselves spiritual is simply to read the Bible and try hard to obey God. It's a good thing to do, but we're able to do it only when we are empowered by the Holy Spirit. Obedience follows being filled with the Spirit, not the other way around.

## What the Filling of the Spirit Is

THE THIRD IDEA I would like to discuss about the Holy Spirit is this, "What the filing of the Holy Spirit really is," because so many ideas swirl around this biblical concept. Some people think they are full of the Spirit when they get excited about God. Now being filled with the Spirit certainly may make you excited about God, but it does not prove that you are full of the Spirit if you are excited. People of other religions get excited about God. On the other hand some people think they are full of the Spirit when they are very active in church, when they are reading their Bible, when they are keeping the commandments they know about.

The key passage in biblical study about the filling of the Spirit is Ephesians 5. The key paragraph begins at verse 15. Notice the end of verse 17 when Paul says, "Understand what the Lord's will is." I learned years ago that we should read the Bible in its context. That means to look at the verses before and after a key verse before you interpret that verse. The verse after verse 17, of course, is verse 18, and verse 18 says, "Do not get drunk on wine, which leads to debauchery. Instead be filled with the Spirit." Although verse 18 is the key verse in this study, verses 19 and following deal with some ideas which we will mention later. They teach what comes after being filled with the Holy Spirit, and they are very important. Verse 18 gives us two commands. One, do not get drunk on wine. Two, be filled with the Spirit. The first command relates to the second command. Believers are told not to get drunk on wine. It's a clear command from God, and no believer should think it's acceptable to be drunk. But the command goes further than that and relates to being filled with the Spirit.

Several parallels relate to being drunk with wine and being filled with the Spirit. First, a person who is drunk with wine has deliberately swallowed the wine which has made him drunk. Similarly, we have to be deliberate about being filled with the Holy Spirit. We have to do some things on purpose. Second, a person drunk on wine is controlled by that wine. He is under the influence of alcohol. In the same way a person who is controlled by the Holy Spirit is under the influence of God, the Holy Spirit. Third, in order to stay drunk on wine an individual has to continue to drink wine. If he doesn't, the effects of the wine will wear off and he will no longer be drunk after awhile. If you and I wish to continue to be filled with the Spirit, we must constantly be submitting ourselves to the Lord and dealing with the Holy Spirit in a biblical way. Don't get drunk on wine. If you are filled with the Holy Spirit, you will not wish to be drunk with wine. I tell people that I get drunk as often as I want to. I never want to!

The second command in this passage is, "Be filled with the Spirit." This straightforward command that God is giving to His children concerns their relationship with the Holy Spirit. As I said earlier, the only way to live the Christian life effectively is to live under the control of the Spirit. Here, I believe, is the key verse in the entire Bible concerning the filling of the Spirit. I don't want to be overly academic in presenting these ideas.

However it is important that we mine all the truth in this key verse. The verb in this phrase be filled with the Spirit is, of course, "be filled," and it contains several important ideas. First of all, it is plural in number, which plainly shows us that God wishes all of us to be filled with the Spirit. Next, it is present in its tense; the idea is always being filled with the Spirit. Yesterday's filling is not adequate for today. Third, it is passive in voice. In other words the subject (you and I) receives the action of the verb. Being filled with the Holy Spirit is not something that you do; it is something you allow God to do. We are passive in that activity. Finally, it is imperative in mood. It's a command from God, not an option. It is not a take it or leave it situation. Here is a command that God expects us to obey. A believer in Jesus Christ is either filled with the Holy Spirit, or he/she is not. This verse could read, "Always allow yourselves to be filled with the Spirit."

The last time I was a full time pastor I lived in Arkansas. There was a young man who was a member of my church. For the first year or so that he attended, he came to our services, watched me closely, studied the Bible as I preached, and did not react much. Then after about a year something dramatic happened in his life, and he was different. What had happened? As we talked about being sold out to Jesus and being filled with the Holy Spirit, he had taken it in. Finally he decided it was for him, and he made a full surrender of his life to Jesus afresh. Suddenly, he was different. He wanted to pray for revival, he wanted to learn how to share his faith in Christ, and he did. The difference in his life came when he submitted his heart to the control of the Holy Spirit, and he allowed Jesus Christ to take control of his heart.

The idea of walking in the Spirit is presented in Galatians 5. Walking in the Spirit is another term for being filled with the Spirit. The idea is simply as you live your life from one step to another you should be filled with the Spirit each step, and as you progress in life you will be walking in the Spirit. This is not a new concept or a new idea in scripture. It's very similar and supplementary to being filled with the Holy Spirit.

Peter Jenkins is a man from New York State, who is about my age (60). He graduated from college in 1973 (the year I graduated from the University of Alabama), and he decided he did not want to get a regular job at that time. He wanted to find out what makes this country tick, what holds it together, and how it is special. So with his dog, he set out from upstate New York and began to walk, meet people, find jobs, and earn his way across the nation. He walked south and found himself in the state of Alabama, and finally in the city of Mobile. One evening Peter Jenkins wandered into an evangelistic crusade where James Robison was preaching. He wanted to take some pictures of the preacher, so he found a place to sit on the ground near the podium. While he was sitting there, the Holy Spirit of God began to work in his heart, and he soon was under conviction of his need for Jesus Christ. When the invitation was given, Peter walked forward and gave his life to Jesus. He continued his walk across America. He was walking and serving the Lord with Jesus in his heart. Even though he may not have known it, he was walking in the Spirit. I discovered Peter Jenkins and his walking through *National Geographic Magazine*. Then I got a copy of his book *Walk Across America* and really enjoyed reading it. Later I heard him speak at the Southern Baptist Convention and found out that he was an intriguing Christian speaker.

Many Christians have not known about being filled with the spirit or walking in the Spirit, and yet they have done both. They have committed their life fully to Jesus as the Lord of their life, and they have found themselves walking in the Spirit although they wouldn't call it that. Whether you realized it or not, if you've been sold out to Jesus, you've been walking in the Spirit. For the rest of your life, join me and let's walk in the Spirit together. Do not allow yourself to just sit and soak at church. Get a job serving the Lord in your local church, and do great things through the power of the Holy Spirit for Jesus Christ!

Several other key passages in the New Testament deal with the Holy Spirit and His filling. One such text is in John 7. Near the end of John 7 there is a discussion about Jesus being in Jerusalem on that "Great day of the feast." This was the feast of the Tabernacles and although Jesus utters only a few words in this passage, it is loaded spiritually. If you really want to be filled with the Holy Spirit listen closely to these words and examine them with me. Four ideas in this passage relate to the filling of the Spirit. First, Jesus says, "If anyone thirsts." You and I will never be full of the Spirit until we are thirsty for God. Of course this is a spiritualized idea about being thirsty. We cannot drink God, but we can have a longing for Him. When I am really thirsty I have a longing for water or something good to drink. The problem with this passage is that so many church members and professed Christians today are satisfied. They think they are spiritually fine. They really cannot relate to the saying of the Marines which states, "The few, the proud, The Marines." Few Christians are thirsty and hungry for God, and few are willing to pay the price to be full of the Holy Spirit. It is useless for us to try to be spiritual people until we are thirsty for the Lord.

The second idea in this passage is when Jesus says, "Come to me." We must be willing to come to Jesus just like He is. He is Lord! He is not our buddy. He is not only our friend, He is Lord. This passage reminds me of Matthew 11:28-30 where Jesus says, "Come to me all you who labor, and are heavy laden, and I will give you rest. Take my yoke upon you." It's very simple to come to Jesus, but we can't come to Jesus with rebellious hearts. We come to Jesus in surrender. We come with His yoke on us. Jesus is the source of the Spirit filled life, He is the one that makes it happen. In Luke 9:23 Jesus said, "If any man wishes to come after me, let him deny himself and take up his cross daily and follow me." The idea in this verse is that a person must be willing to come to Jesus as a follower, and he must be willing to die to his own desires so he can obey Jesus. I'm not speaking about trying to be like Jesus, I'm talking about surrendering to Jesus, because He is the source of the Spirit-filled life.

The third idea in this passage in John is also in verse 37 where Jesus says, "And drink." What is the idea in this statement? Here the Lord is talking about taking action concerning our spiritual life. In other words, we need to believe and then do. We will never be Spirit filled Christians until we act upon the promises of God, and ask the Lord to fill us with the Holy Spirit. Luke 11:13 states, "If you then, being evil, know how to give good gifts to your children, how much more will your heavenly Father give the Holy Spirit to those who ask him?" (NKJV) In a very straightforward manner the Lord Jesus tells us to ask Him for the Holy Spirit. We must ask Him to control our lives by the Spirit after we have met His conditions as discussed above. We must surrender, we must keep our heart clean of known sin, and then we must ask him to fill us with the Holy Spirit.

The fourth idea in the passage from John 7 is in verse 38 where Jesus said, "He who believes in Me as the Scripture has said, out of his heart will flow rivers of living water." What is this "rivers of living water"? One of my best friends has done mission work along the Amazon for over a decade. In the city of Tefe, Brazil, he has been allowed to preach to thousands of people during Carnival. Carnival is similar to Mardi Gras. Usually he takes a team of 10 to 20 people with him, and they fly into Manaus, Brazil, catch a river boat and go four to five hundred miles west on the Amazon River. They normally go in the rainy season because the Amazon will be high and they will be able to get to the river banks, and thus to the villages to preach the gospel. Some places on the Amazon at flood time are more than 30 miles wide across the river. A person could stand on one side of the Amazon at this place and not be able to see the other bank across the river. The earth curves and we can see less than 30 miles. That's a lot of river.

Jesus said there will be rivers of living water flowing from us. You can imagine that nobody would even think about damning the Amazon River when it is 30 miles wide. In a similar sense and in a spiritual way nobody can stop the living water which comes from our lives to touch the lives of other people and accomplish the will of God. Those who are controlled by the Holy Spirit have the power of God flowing from them. This river of living water is similar to what Paul talks about in 2 Corinthians 2:14 when he says that Christ, "through us diffuses the fragrance of His knowledge in every place" (NKJV). That's the living water that's flowing from us when we are full of the Holy Spirit.

How do we get filled with the Holy Spirit? We have to be a Christian, and we have to have a thirst and hunger for God. We must be willing to turn from any known sin in our life and repent of it. We must be willing to surrender, and we must surrender everything to Jesus. Then we must ask God to fill us with His Spirit. It's not a formula, it's just a lifestyle. It is in the Bible, it is for you and me, and it is for today. If you want to live a Christian life, you have to be filled with the Holy Spirit!

What about the results of being filled with the Spirit? First of all in a selfish way, let me tell you that it is delightful and that much joy comes when you are controlled by the Holy Spirit. Joy; everybody on earth wants to have joy in their life. The only biblical way to have joy is to be full of the Spirit of God, because joy is a fruit of the Holy Spirit. Another result of being filled with the Spirit is the fruit of the Spirit. In Galatians 5:22 and 23, the Bible lists nine fruit of the Holy Spirit. You will notice the term is fruit, not fruits, because it's a package deal. You either have them all, or you don't have any of them. If you're controlled by the Holy Spirit, you have the fruit of the Spirit. In other words you have all nine of them. You have love, joy, peace, patience, kindness, goodness, faithfulness, gentleness, and self-control. It's simply a result of being filled with the Spirit.

Some people think speaking in tongues is a direct result of being filled with the Spirit. The first relationship that I ever had with a charismatic Christian was when I was a summer Youth Director at a Mississippi church in 1972. A young man who looked like a hippie was in our church. His name was Mike, and he really loved Jesus Christ. In fact he told me that he had only been a Christian for 5 months, and it seemed that he knew the

New Testament better than I did. Mike lived in a communal house that was called the "Jesus house." It was toward the end of the Jesus movement. and the movement had really hit in West Point, Mississippi. Mike and I had several good discussions about Jesus and the Bible. He brought me a book and I remember being afraid of that book as if it was going to bite me. I knew that he was Charismatic, but I didn't know much about that. I was afraid that I might catch it! Mike and those like him were tongue speakers. They believed that one of the fruits of being filled with the Holy Spirit was to speak in an unknown tongue.

I have studied this issue since about 1972, and for the last 26 years I have taught courses that have allowed me to dig even further into these issues. I am thoroughly convinced that speaking in tongues is a biblical practice. The word in the original language for tongue was *glossa* and it simply means our physical tongue or a spoken language. The Greek word *dialectos* means dialect. Those two words are used in the New Testament when talking about tongues. Of course tongues occurred in the New Testament, but tongues were always languages in Acts 2. When the Holy Spirit came on the day of Pentecost, the languages were spoken. Christians were enabled to speak in languages they had not learned, and people who did not know certain languages were able to hear them in their own languages—a supernatural occurrence. Today the gift of tongues still exists and still occurs, but only in rare situations.

I have looked far and wide in devotional and biographical books and have only found 3 instances of biblical tongue speaking. All of them relate to a person speaking to another person who speaks a different language. The first person is speaking his own language and is able to speak in a supernatural way in the language of another. Occasionally God enables someone to speak a language they haven't learned so they too can share the gospel. That is the purpose of tongues, and that is what the Bible teaches. Of course all Christians don't agree with me, and I have learned that this not an issue that I wish to argue or debate. I love Christians who are on both sides of this issue, but what I have stated above seems to be the biblical perspective on tongues.

So tongues are not something that happens because one is full of the Holy Spirit. In Ephesians 5, after the passage which talks about being filled with the Spirit, the passage offers several clear results of being filled with the Spirit. In Ephesians 5:19, we are told how to speak to one another. One result of being filled with the Spirit is that we speak to other people in a nice and kind way. The second part of verse 19 mentions making music in our heart to the Lord. This is a picture of joy—singing in our heart. Verse 20 mentions another result, it says that we should always be giving thanks to God, or we should have the "attitude of gratitude" for everything in the name of Jesus. Then verse 21 tells how we are to submit to one another. I have learned that one of the keys to help women submit to men in their marriage relationship is for the man to have a submissive spirit to the woman first. It doesn't mean that the man is not the head of the home. It means that he is submissive in spirit to his wife. He listens to her, and tries to do what she wants. Submission is a result of being filled with the Holy Spirit. In verse 22 women are told to submit to their husbands. Certainly this can only be done correctly when wives are full of the Spirit. Finally in verse 25 husbands are told to love their wives as Christ loved the church. That submission too is a result of being filled with the Spirit. Christian marriage works when there are Spirit filled partners in the marriage.

Through the study of these Bible passages, I am ending this book on what I believe is the highest note in the Christian life—that of being filled with the Holy Spirit. I am quick to tell you that the Spirit-filled life is not a panacea—it is not a cure all. However, it is the key that unlocks and makes the Christian life make sense. I would urge you to pay attention to all the chapters in this short book, but I would particularly urge you to study the Spirit filled life. Two main themes dominate the Bible. The first theme is how a person can be right with God, or how they can be saved. The second theme is how the Christian believer can walk with God, and serve Him here on earth. Christianity is not just for the future, it is also for the now. My prayer for you is that you will be a joyful, serving, witnessing, Spirit filled Christian. It is the only way to go!

# About the Author

STEVE WILKES is a professor in the Department of Missions at Mid-America Baptist Theological Seminary and is the Editor of the *Journal of Evangelism and Missions.* He is also President of World-Wide Church Planters, a group that helps to start churches in responsive areas of the world.

He has served in the ministry for over 39 years and has spent 26 years teaching Baptist ministers.

CPSIA information can be obtained at www.ICGtesting.com
Printed in the USA
LVOW12s1434011113
359624LV00020B/928/P